HEALING

WHILE

PARENTING

The Hardest Thing You Will Ever Do - A Mother's True Story Detailing The Steps Taken to Transcend Early Trauma and Find Peace of Mind

SHANTELLE SINACOLA

This book is dedicated to my healing team, my mother, my best friend Erica, my husband, and my children. Without their listening and their patience, I would not have survived, let alone be here to tell the story.

CONTENTS

CHAPTER ONE

CHAPTER TWO

CHAPTER THREE

CHAPTER FOUR

CHAPTER FIVE

CHAPTER SIX

CHAPTER SEVEN

CHAPTER EIGHT

CHAPTER NINE

CHAPTER TEN

Foreword

This book is by no means claiming, to be the first ever account, detailing the connections and consequences, of a past riddled with trauma and challenges. Nor the first to detail, the subsequent parents that these experiences create. This is merely the story, of how I personally came to understand the journey.

At best, I want to connect with other people, that are struggling to work on themselves, while parenting. If nothing else, I want this story to cause a separation, between you, and the things that are in the way of your peace.

CHAPTER ONE

Ordinary Life

THE FIRST TIME I REMEMBER

The very first memory I had as a child was at the age of five Years old. I was lying in my bed; when I started to become aware that I was in a dream state, the awareness arose in the sudden feeling of falling. I was falling deeply and slowly back down to where my fragile body lay.

I heard noises. At first, it sounded like I was underwater, the voices were indistinct, and the words blended. The sound became louder; I wished it would stop. I did not fully understand the words that were being shouted, but the context quickly revealed itself to me. Words of anger, rage, and cries of pain travelled through my ear canals and waged war on my soul. My body started to shake as though cold hands had just disturbed my warmth; I let out a long cry of "Mum." That was the first

1

time I remember feeling the heaviness of this world. This outburst was met with a deep and determined 'go back to sleep' from my dad. I did as I was told to do.

That night was the night of firsts; it was also the first time I put my fingers deep in my ears. The coping mechanism of clenching my ears and forbidding sounds of pain from entering, would serve me well for the next ten years. My mum and I lived in a micro-society, and my dad was our owner. Just as a disobedient worker would be sanctioned, when my mum did things that my dad deemed wrong, she was given consequence, only in her case, it was not a verbal or written warning but physical punishment.

It was not hard coming to the micro-society conclusion. I knew early on that there would more than likely be a physical consequence if you did something wrong. In the early days of my childhood, it would be a smacked bum as he bent me over his hard knee; eventually, it would be the old-fashioned net curtain rods, belts, and wires. Sudden rage in him could even deliver me a clenched fist. Once, this rage appeared because I had only achieved nine correct spellings out of ten in a primary school test.

In fear, I always tried my best not to do anything wrong. I could not understand why my mum would do 'wrong' things so often and by mistake. I did not even know what those 'wrong' things were half of the time, not in the early days anyway. Why would she take the risk of angering him, knowing what would happen?

Despite these questions that I had, I loved her dearly, and she was my world. I knew that my mother had a beautiful heart. As a young child, I sometimes wondered if she realised the pain, it caused me, to hear her being hurt (I realised as I matured, that she had no control over this violence). Sometimes I would hear in her tone that she was not fully intoxicated by forced alcohol. During these sober times, she tried her best to suffer quietly so that I would not hear, but I still did. I looked at her as you would an angel, captured in a glass jar by an evil king, whose sole mission in life was to break her spirit so she could not fly away.

By the time I hit double figures in age, I had fully realised his game. He was a drinker; but I do not know if he was an alcoholic. Everyone that met him concluded that he was charming, articulate, and intelligent. My dad drank mostly at night. He would put music on and proceed to ply my mother with alcohol; she was not allowed to say no to it. The drink, the music, the darkness of the night, and his soul, delivered feelings of dread for my mother and me.

My mum knew that there would be consequences she could not control for both her and my dad. She knew that his evil would become unapologetically intoxicated, and his hate would rampage. She knew that she would become brave. This combination would bring bloodshed, and it would not be his. She knew that no one would come to save her and that her child would hear the bloodshed and see the wounds. She knew that her child would kiss her on her forehead and tell her that everything would be ok in the end.

The younger me did not understand the connection with the alcohol; I thought that when my dad attacked my mum, she would become this fiery warrior who could not help but fight back. All the while, I wished that she would just back down. I prayed that she would behave, but on those alcohol-fuelled nights, she never did; she always delivered what he wanted, which was a reason to hurt her.

I cannot pinpoint precisely when I began to see myself and my mum as a team; however, it was early on. Our micro-society was run by a dictatorship that the rest of the world was not privy to. We ate, slept, spoke, drank, and washed when he instructed that we could. We lived in fear of breaking the rules, rules that we sometimes did not even know existed.

There were islands within our micro-society to keep us further separated. My siblings and I were prisoners, locked behind doors with the handles removed, signs of affection from a mother to her children forbidden. Whispers carrying words of 'goodnight' and 'I Love you' travel in quiet breath from one island to the next. Our closeness formed from the constant navigation between what we were allowed to do and what we were not. We were kept worlds apart, but this is what made us feel close.

The rest of the world seemed so far away from my mother and me. The separation was not by land or water but by fear and lack of will. We lived in a flat six stories high, but we might as well have lived on the moon. There was no hope of anyone ever coming to help; other people did not exist to us. We were around people, I went to school, and she went to work, but they could never reach us, and we could not reach out to them.

We had neighbours to the side of us and neighbour's underneath. None of them saw fit to extend a helping hand. All we received from those neighbours were sad, glances of guilt as we passed by one another on the stairwell. The neighbours knew. The beatings were never quiet and often happened late at night when there was little outside noise to explain our predicament away. The neighbours never came; they never alerted the police or child protection, not that the police were concerned with domestic issues during the eighties.

My mum had one night managed to flee the flat, barefooted, and bloody; she had run the two blocks to the police station, swiftly followed by my dad, who then fed the police a story about her being drunk and crazy. I cannot imagine how she felt in that horrific moment, having to turn around and walk back to her fate with my dad. She, like so many other times, was barely alive the next day.

MECHANICS

I had gone onto the balcony to watch people go by. After a while, I began to hear my dad's voice. Octaves were flowing upward as he began to release that which had been building up in him.

The feeling of dread started making its way down from my thoughts to its resting place, and the inevitable sick feeling made manifest in my stomach. Heavy footsteps began to travel towards the balcony door. It was a bizarre feeling; it was as if all of life's background noise had become obsolete. The sound of the key turning in the lock now replaced the chaos of the passing traffic. Each cog connected with the next like the scene that was slowly unfolding.

We were all part of the mechanics, the only difference being that the key knew its end goal; my dad did not. He operated from impulse alone. In the beginning, he dreamt of power and dominance, but he had achieved this long ago. My dad was now left with an insatiable thirst for a fight. It was the only way he knew to relieve himself of the rage that was resident within him. He locked the door.

I do not know why he locked me out there. He had thought that there was a chance that I would come running in to try and save her. I did not dare do such things in general; however, my anger did once get the better of me.

One night, I was on the top bunk bed in my room, trying to bury my fingers deeper into my ears. I was unsuccessful; the sound still managed to penetrate. My bedroom was at the end of a hallway, and my door had a glass window above it. That night, I had had enough, so I stood up on my bed.

To my horror, I was greeted with the image of my mum running down the hallway, face bloody. I shouted with all that I had in me, 'leave her alone!' My voice became more profound, older, and not afraid. Years of frustrations came bursting through me. My dad's eyes had met with mine, and as the last syllable left my mouth, he came bursting in. He threw me from the top bunk bed onto the hard floor. I knew where my place was, and I knew there was little that I could do to help.

Back on the balcony, as the key completed its mission, I unknowingly began mine. The shouting became louder, and so did the screams and the bangs. I frantically looked up and down the street, leaning over the cold metal railing, to see if there was anyone I could call out to for help; the road was desolate.

Directly outside of our flats was a bus stop. A bus had just pulled up. The bus did not open its doors, and the engine continued running. I decided that I would have to get the bus driver, but how? If I shouted for help, surely my dad would hear me and stop me. I doubted that the bus driver would even hear me with the bus doors closed. There was only one thing to do.

While meditating on my lack of confidence not too long ago, I was taken back to this balcony event; this time, however, it looked quite different. I was able to view this event through the lenses of a new perspective. I used to describe this event as 'I decided to jump off the balcony to get the bus driver to help my mum. Crazy, right?'

This time, during meditation, I saw a new picture. I saw that fear had vanished and left behind an overpowering need to save her. I jumped.

As I fell to the ground, I felt free, not just because of the motion but because of the will in the choice. Later that day, I would recall peacefully watching a bird perched in a tree that seemed to be also watching me. I fell softly to the ground and landed on the grass with no more than a thud. I lay there for a short while, looking up at the soft blue sky just above the balcony that I had just left.

As my gaze dropped slightly and my eyes arrived back at the balcony, disbelief hit me; I could not believe that I had jumped and survived. I looked at the window and was quickly brought back to the reality of why I had jumped in the first place. I sat upright and looked at the bus behind me. I tried to stand up shakily and failed.

A man with long, aged dreadlocks pulled up on his bicycle. The man got off his bike and walked the short distance across the grass to where I had softly landed. He crouched down, lowering himself to my eye level, and asked me if I was okay. I was still disoriented but aware enough to see the genuine kindness in his eyes.

I pointed up at our balcony and told him that I had jumped. I explained that I jumped because I needed to get someone to come and help my mum, who was being beaten up. I watched confusion and disbelief dance across his face; it formed lines of coherence that refused to join.

The kind man scooped me up, placed me on his handlebars, and declared that we were going to the police station. I allowed a spark of hope to enter me. In jumping, I had unwittingly brought us all to the threshold. This would be the event that breached the barrier between us and the rest of the world.

I assumed that because I was a child, the police would take this whole event very seriously. It was my chance to save us. No one could blame my accounts for being drunk or crazy. I began to build up a picture in my mind of how the police would receive me.

I allowed myself to imagine the police rushing around for me, or detectives looking furious listening to my account of an evil villain. I imagined a detective in a brown suit with a crisp white unforgiving shirt slamming a caseload on a desk. The detective declares, 'don't worry sweetheart, we will get your mum' before storming out of the station with twenty other officers in tow. We would be saved and live happily ever after.

When I described the violence and why I had jumped, I was met with sterile faces that recorded each of my words in isolation as I spoke them. My heart sat back down, slummed in hopeless. The police transferred me to the children's hospital, located conveniently next to the police station. At the hospital, a caring nurse with a strong Jamaican accent checked over my body. After my check-up, the nurse asked me what had happened. After I finished recalling the event, the nurse, with a warm smile and raised eyebrows, confidently told me that the bird I had been watching while I was falling was my guardian angel.

The nurse said that she knew I was protected because all I had sustained was a sprained ankle. I found this notion hard to believe. Why would I be saved while falling from a balcony but not when beaten by a grown man? The nurse continued to say that coincidentally, the man that scooped me up onto his bike was her son.

The police contacted my parents, who were then interviewed together. My dad told them that he did not lock the door and that they were watching an adult film with loud violence. Mum had no other option but to corroborate.

When I look back at this event now, at thirty-nine years old, I see it as the bravest thing I have ever done instead of the craziest. I tried to be a hero in real life. Although it has been buried for decades, underneath the struggle to survive, I still have that same spirit and need to help others. Eventually, I will need to jump again. However, this time, it will be off the edge of my comfort zone and into the cosmic sea of potential.

NIGHT SCHOOL

My only surviving memories are like snapshots of critical first times or extremes. Most 'normal' childhood memories died in the war, and they were the forgotten soldiers that fought for hope. Rarely, a fond memory tries to come through. I try to catch it, but it quickly fades like a ghost that cannot rest. General trauma was ordinary and deemed far too insignificant to be allocated memory space.

It would be the same as someone else, not holding space in their memory for the daily family breakfasts that they had every morning as a child. That person may recall the one hilarious morning when the milk was off, all the eggs in the carton were all damaged, and on retrieval of a slice of bread, had found instead a moist, squishy, square of green mould. They remember this morning because they decided to go out for an impromptu breakfast feast at the local café. For years to come, I would hold onto my trauma like a child would hold its parent's hand in fear.

Trauma was my foundation. Having consistency at all was good for me as a child; it meant that I could plan.

I am unsure about how old I was when my dad started to take an interest in me. I know I was small because I was able to sit on his knee, feeling engulfed with my legs dangling. During the early years, my dad would wake me up in the middle of the night and tell me that we were going to have a special time. For me, these nights were extra special; they were unusually quiet. On these nights, I was able to get a good few hours' sleep. There was no shouting or screaming, or voiceless thuds against the wall. It was peaceful because he knew he had other plans.

My mum would be let off the hook for the night and allowed to rest. Little did she know that her rest was my shift. He would lead me down the hall and into the living room. He would then take the handle off the door, which was not unusual for him to do.

My dad made it feel like I was having a treat by being up so late. I was young and naive enough not to see anything sinister in his actions; if anything, I was confused and curious. I knew I was not about to be hit or spanked because the atmosphere told me so. I had no hate for him as a young child because I had nothing to compare to; it was as it was.

I vividly remember the first time that he revealed his prize possession to me, his sexual organs. He told me biologically what the various parts were and what they were for. He would guide my delicate hands in exploring these new lands. He presented himself as an instructor just doing his job. I was still innocent and unaware, the perfect student.

Throughout the years, he made it seem as though he was helping me to learn the things that I would have to learn anyway. My night-time education included body investigations and practical's. My theory lessons took place sitting on his knee, on an old tartan checked recliner chair, in front of the TV watching pornography. As I began to grow, my changing body unwittingly sent signals of incitement to my dad. Soon I would be ready.

During our years in the flat, he did everything with me but full intercourse; that is not saying that he did not try. I was too skinny and small for him. Each time he tried; he would cause me extreme pain. He did not want me to be in obvious pain because he could not maintain the 'special time' charade.

In the coming years, he would lose the need to justify the abuse. By double digits, I was considered a woman. My dad needed new boundaries to cross, and fresh psyches to crush. He needed to feel the challenge again and the enviable release of serotonin after succeeding. It was a long-term project, but it was worth it. He had already broken every part of my mum. The hunt for her now lacked the lustre it once did. She barely even ran anymore, so he needed the young meat in me.

DID YOU KNOW THAT LIES FLOAT?

One night when I was around eight years old, my dad crept into my room. I slowly gained consciousness as he gently tapped on the back of my flowery nightie. He signalled for me to follow him and led me to the kitchen. I was bewildered and had assumed in my daze that it was a 'special time,' however, I quickly realised that this was not the case.

When we arrived in the kitchen, I noticed that he had filled the sink with glistening water. The look on his face slowly started to reveal itself; it said 'sorry.' My dad told me that he had a feeling that I had told him a lie.

My adult spiritual journey has enabled me to describe my initial experience that night, more accurately. While my body prepared to flight, my soul cowered in my stomach as it awaited what was to come.

People often report leaving their bodies when trauma is happening to them; I was not so lucky in this instance. I told him that I had not told any lies, he said he was sorry, but he did not believe that to be true. He told me that he would have to put my head under the water until I told him the lie, and if I did not tell him, I would drown. He said that when I drown, the lies would float to the top of the water, and all would be well.

The immediate response was panic. I do not know why I did not think just to tell him what he wanted to hear. Maybe if it had been in waking hours, I would have managed it better. I would have pre-empted the situation in waking hours and assessed what I could do to help it.

I pleaded with him to believe me, asking him, why would I dare lie? But he would not listen. He had an agenda, and he was going to see it through. He put his hand around the back of my neck and slowly pushed my head down into the water.

As I wrote this, I felt like a part of this event was missing, which I had neglected to describe. Where is the section in which I describe my dad tying my hands behind my back or how he held my thin wrists? I went back to the event in deep meditation and tried to recall how and if my wrists were bound.

I re-emerge back into the scene as he pushes my head into the water. I felt the compressed hardness of the metal underneath my hands; I was holding the sides of the sink. My hands were not bound. I was shocked and saddened. The revelation portrayed a stark picture of what it was like to be a prisoner of an abusive household. It was not the walls that held you firmly in place but the mental conditioning, forcing you to believe that you would never be free.

He did not need to restrain me or tie my hands because they were already bound. He did not need to gag me because I would never dare call for help. Who would come if I did? The neighbours who had never bothered before. The police who had once turned my mum away, bruised, and scared? My Mum? And then I would suffer twice fold having to listen to her receiving punishment for attempting to intervene. There was no one coming to save me.

The water was lukewarm against the cold of the sink. My head was under the water for fifteen seconds before he let me back up. He asked me again, 'what lies have you told?' I tell him again that I have not told any, and I beg him to believe me. I tried to appeal to his compassion even though he had never shown any before.

He pushed my head back under the water again, this time for two0 seconds. When he let me up, he repeated, 'what lies have you told?' I told him with all the conviction in my heart, 'none!' This time when he pushed my head back in, he did not pull it out as quick. I struggled under the water and tried to rise through my arms. He had pushed his body firmly over mine like a heavy anchor keeping a ship in place.

It was an eternity under that water, then came the calm. I stopped struggling, and I opened my eyes. Black dots of dizziness came together, and I felt like I was falling to the bottom of an abyss. It was peaceful and quiet. I had taken a small step towards the end; the water held a promise, and I only had to ask to redeem it. I was about to die, and I was not afraid. As the last traces of oxygen left me, my chest tightened, and my heartbeat fast and deep, the sound like tribal and trance. It was calling me home, and I was ready to let go.

As the darkness fully engulfed me, my dad pulled me out. He asked me one more time, 'what lies have you told?' This time I thought for a minute, I thought about the peace I had just felt and how I could be finished with this life. I did not need to be here. I was of no real importance to my mum or siblings. Realistically, I could do nothing to help or save them, so why should I stay?

Pictures appeared in my mind of stolen kisses and whispered plans of freedom between my mum and me. The love we still managed to feel amid the evil was a miracle. I cry like a baby whenever I think about the hundreds of millions of children worldwide that grow up in households where both parents are violent and abusive.

As a society, we have a lot to answer for, we cannot even see past our own lives to protect our most vulnerable. I knew at that moment that the joining of my small light and the tiny light my mum had left slowly nourished a small but potent seed of hope that we all needed. I told him what he wanted to hear, I admitted to a lie, I do not remember what I said, and it does not matter. All that mattered was that I had to surrender.

My dad told me to dry off and go back to bed as though nothing had ever happened. I have since researched this theory of his about the lies and the water. I found out that the idea was based on a quote. The quote says, 'truth is like oil, no matter how much water you use to depress it, it will always float to the top.'

PERSPECTIVE MY SUPERPOWER

We ran away from that section of our lives when I was eleven years old. My mum took us to a women's refuge. This refuge was the second one we had been to and the first one that I remembered. It was a unique experience, a wonderful time. We were finally free.

During that time in the refuge, I met a wonderful Indian boy who introduced me to Bollywood music, and I danced and laughed. The smells and tastes of the exotic spices from his mum's cooking were divine.

The refuge was extremely comfortable. It was a big house with multiple rooms. There, soft furnishings, compassion, and a wonderful playground with swings lived. I spent my days on those swings, staring happily up at a new piece of sky.

Most importantly, it was safe. My mum and my siblings were now able to show each other love without fear freely. Imagine living a life where safety is a privilege.

To feel free was a wonderful experience. To express myself in words of my own choice, anytime I wanted, and to be able to speak truthfully was a massive relief. A potential was born in that refuge, that one day I may find out who I was.

It had only been three weeks before he found us, and just like that, the holiday was over. I could not believe that he found us. It was after this event that I realised that his power stretched far beyond our household. He was handsome, charming, brilliant, and could manipulate anything out of anyone. We were found and once again captured.

Going back to live with him was terrifying because I now knew the extent of his reach. Before this capture, there was always the dream and the sometimes-inconceivable hope of escape. I could no longer see even a glimpse of light at the end of the tunnel.

Unfortunately, on this occasion, he had used my grandparents. It was not until years later, decades even, that I found out that he had jumped through my grandparent's window with a knife and threatened to take their lives if they did not tell him where we were. They did not have an exact address for us, but they could relay the message. As soon as my mum found out the length that he was willing to go, we were on our way back.

The return home took longer because we got a new house, creating a fake sense of a fresh start. He told her that things would be different. It was not long, before the new house was christened with my mum's punishment for leaving in the first place. This attack was to be the second of three horrendous beatings given to my mum by my dad. All three beatings were savage and left her out of sight and in her room, recovering for a long time.

The first of these beatings took place in the flat before we left for the refuge. I do not know what she did to warrant almost death, but I did catch a glimpse of her face, and it made me feel sick. When her body and face had healed sufficiently enough to leave her room, she was allowed to go to the shop. I was to accompany her, and at that time, I was maybe nine years old. On our way to the shop, I remember her asking me to check her scalp for her. She bent her head down so I could see as I carefully parted different sections of her thick curly red hair. I quickly found out why she had asked me to check it. There was a piece of black glass stuck in her scalp. It was the black glass of our hexagonal dinner plates. The part that was exposed was a 3D square shape. I gently pulled it out, watching it taper into a shard. My stomach churned, and anger boiled. I tried my best not to portray how I felt. She was calm, and matter of fact, I hugged and kissed her. She smiled and said that she was ok.

The second beating was in the new house and awarded to her for leaving in the first place. It followed a similar routine; she was locked away in her room for a week or so.

I had not long started high school. We spent three years in the new house. Although it was a fresh start, it was the exact old story in a different house with the same non-bothered neighbours. The only difference was that I was becoming more proactive in trying to protect my mum.

I was older and wiser during this phase. There were naturally fewer beatings for me. I want to say that was because there were fewer mistakes. The latter was partly true, but it was more so because my dad was now unapologetically having full intercourse with me. I lost my virginity at around ten. Full intercourse did not become a regular thing until the new house.

At around eleven, I had received my period. He told me how disgusting periods are and that if he were to ever wake me up during my period, he would let me know beforehand. I was to get in the bath and scrub myself down below with a stiff bristle brush to ensure I was clean for him for that night. One night, he demonstrated how I was to clean myself and scrubbed me down below so hard that my skin blistered.

On reflection, this was one of the reasons, along with the repressed emotions, that I had such negative menstruations. I blamed my hormones and my body, but it was the past fighting to be felt. During my young adult years, once a month, I raged, cried, argued with people, and had immeasurable pain in my cramps.

When we moved into the new house, things stepped up a pace. He seemed more ok with what he was doing to me each year that I became older. Despite this, he still covered his tracks. When my period started, he told me that I had to wear different clothes around the house. According to him, I was becoming more of a woman now.

He once bought me a red pleated mini skirt and told me to wear it as often as possible. I remember this skirt because it was rare that I got new clothes. He explained away this change in attire by pretending that he was letting me dress how I wanted. I played along, but I knew that it was not right. I was in high school now and had observed how the other girls spoke about their families and their dads.

I vowed to do anything I could to protect my mum. This newfound protection I gave included pouring his alcohol, Brandy, or whiskey, down the sink and topping it up with water. The protection I could give my mum also included not only cooperating when he woke me up at night and pretending that I did not hate every second of it. On rare occasions, I even went as far as encouraging him to wake me up.

I did this when I felt his anger brewing, and I could sense her fear. I would quietly ask him if I could stay up late. I did not want it, I wanted to be a child, but it was all I could do to help her. I was able to compare the two pains, and there was no comparison. Hearing my mother being beaten to a pulp was unbearable for me. It was a million times worse than having to lay underneath his heavy, sweaty body, frozen pretending I was ok.

CHAPTER TWO

❦

The End

JUST LIKE THAT SHE WAS GONE

I had been at school all day and had returned home. I was greeted with the image of my little siblings sitting around our big white circular dining table, and my dad stood staring into the distance. I do not speak of my siblings often in this book because I do not have early memories of them. I was not only a prisoner of the micro-society but also of my mind, I spent countless days and nights locked in a bedroom with my siblings, yet I might as well of been in solitary confinement.

I was so preoccupied with assessing my environment, predicting atmospheres, and reading between the lines that I was never fully present for my siblings. I did not remember any babies in our house. I do not remember my mum's swollen belly or stroking it, wondering about the new life within her.

I was standing at the front door trying to focus on the scene; it was difficult because I was spinning internally. The spinning slowed down, and I began moving backwards, in slow motion. The scene stopped and started again. I had felt normal as I had approached my front door. I had entered my key into the lock with my heart maintaining a regular beat. I had pushed the door open and stepped inside. My ears took control, listening for sound as I always did on returning home. It was silent. One step, two steps, three steps, and I was inside.

My dad is stood up. He seemed to be hiding agitation behind the blank wall of his face. I glanced at my siblings sitting at the dining table, and then back to him. My heart sank. I wanted to return to the beginning of the scene again, but this time pause it forever. He told me to sit down.

I could hear him, but it sounded distorted like I was underwater; my young mind was racing. As my body hits the seat, I was jolted into the present, and I was suddenly awake.

My dad said the words, 'your mum has left.' I was grateful for the rigid plastic seat beneath me. My legs would have had little chance of supporting me as my world fell apart.

My dad told me that my mum had gone and that he did not know where. I was in shock. He then added that 'she had better not have done something stupid and if she has, she had better hope that he did not find her.' Fear had covered me in its blanket, wrapping itself around me tighter and tighter, I felt smothered, and I could not breathe. Questions shot through my mind like bullets from a gun, where was she? Had she managed to get away? Why would she leave me with him?

I knew my mum would not run away without us. She may, however, have decided not just to leave this nightmare but this earth. He looked at me and told me that we are to stay exactly where we are until he returns and that he was going to find her and bring her back.

The minute he left; I fell into frantic prayer to an entity I was still unsure even existed.

I begged, 'Please, please, let her be dead, please GOD, do not let her come back here, not just for her sake but for ours.' I could not take anymore. I could no longer bear witness to her hell and his evilness. I chanted prayers repeatedly for hours; we sat at that table, only moving to go to the toilet. The actual implications of her being dead did not cross my mind, I just wanted her to be free. She deserved to be free.

The thought of what he would do with me without her here did not cross my mind. The things he would do with my sister as she got older did not cross my mind. How my brother would develop as a man, with him as the only parent did not cross my mind.

I knew why she had gone; the violence had already reached its peak, and she knew she was going to die soon. She had decided that he had taken enough from her. She would not let him take her last breath. Perhaps she had decided that she would instead go on her own terms. She had nothing else left.

I had heard my mum scream, 'just finish it,' many times. At this point, even death was a privilege; he knew it and used it. Death was a privilege not awarded to those captured individuals whose masters liked to feed off the suffering. I knew if he found her, she would come closer to the place she longed for, than ever before.

Unfortunately for her, she would only be beaten until just before her death, nothing more and nothing less. I was around thirteen at this point and had spent my whole life asking, 'why her?' and 'why me?' I sat at that table for what felt like days, the daylight eventually gave in to the night and let the darkness fall.

The front door made a sound; Gravity was pulling me to the ground. The weight of what might be, was too much. He triumphantly walked in with her trailing behind. A smug, accomplished look adorned his face. She sheepishly gives me a fake smile, trying to convey reassurance that she is ok. For a second, I hated her. She wore a hospital band around her wrist.

She had been unsuccessful in her plight. I remember her telling me that she was found by a stranger lying on a park bench, barely conscious after overdosing on medication. She had been taken to hospital and had received a stomach pumping.

He told her to go up to the bedroom. I began to crumble inside. I experienced the most profound sadness that night, not just because of the violence but because my mum was robbed of the most fundamental right, to choose whether to live or die. She had no free will.

My dad looked at me and said, 'you know what has to happen?' He spent the next three days making her wish she had achieved her goal. Those three days were hell on earth. I felt it would never end. The cries and the pain penetrated my whole body and would haunt me for years to come.

I hated myself for not being able to help her more. The worry weight on my shoulders was so heavy that I barely ever looked up. I do not know why I felt responsible for an adult, but I did. I wanted to fight, but there was never any chance of winning. The frustration I felt as a child was immeasurable, I had the fire in my belly but no tools to forge.

DEATH

My mum was living on borrowed time. Living on the borrowed time of a violent partner is different from living on the natural borrowed time of life, that sometimes comes to collect before due time.

When living on the borrowed time of a violent partner void of compassion and morals, there is no time to appreciate your last days or even your last hours; when they come to collect, they make you pay heavily and slowly.

When you live on the borrowed time of a violent partner, you are stuck in your mental and physical prison, living in fear, right up until your last breath. You and those around you may know that your time is running out, but nothing can be done because nothing is set in stone.

If you owed your last days to an illness, you might be gifted with advanced knowledge. You may play with your kids/grandkids. You may stare at them and imagine what kind of beautiful lives they will live. You might lay on the grass on your stomach, observing each glade and the universe within. You might bask in the sun and get drenched in the rain. You may just lay in your hospital bed, silently holding your loved one's hands. These possibilities are void for those who are collateral damage in someone else's life.

I woke up this day as I did every morning, and it started as it always did—nothing special, nothing different. I was still here, and so was she; another night had been survived.

My dad left the house. I know it was the summer holidays because there was no school. I do not know where he went, but as soon as he left my mum started acting funny. Although there were only small, unimportant movements that she was making, I sensed a slight urgency in them. She did not make eye contact with me but threw random gazes at the front door. Was she expecting him to come back? After an hour had passed, she suddenly became frantic, like she had just been turned on like a switch.

She now hurried around faster, trying to find things. She came down the stairs and went into the kitchen. She opened the cupboard under the sink and pulled out a glorious roll of black bags. She allowed herself to take a minute, she used that minute to look at me, and she smiled. Adrenalin started to pump through my body as she spoke the words we are leaving.' She continued to race against the clock, gathering everything we could fit into a black bag while carefully selecting essential items. I sat in the excitement for a while, not allowing myself to think- I did not want to acknowledge the fact that this would be nothing more than another holiday, and when he found us, which he always did, he would most probably kill her.

She called a taxi, and it arrived quickly. We got into the car and began our journey. I stared out the window at the people moving around on the streets going about their daily lives. As I locked eyes with a stranger, I wondered what they would think if they knew that the woman and child staring out of the taxi window smiling albeit cautiously, were fleeing from a real-life horror story. I stopped staring at people when I remembered eye contact was not really for those running away. The next set of eyes you landed on could be those of your captor, as would happen in movies.

She did not tell me where we were going, so I scanned the environment for clues. She did not speak much after we left the house. She had been holding her breath since our departure, waiting for the moment that she felt it was ok to exhale.

The feeling of the car slowing, dragged me out of my thoughts. I could not believe it. There it stood. It could well have been the pearly gates of heaven as far as I was concerned. It was the coach station. The old grey arch was lit up, with yellow fading neon lights spelling coach station. It was beautiful.

Things were suddenly different; now, I was seriously excited. Arriving here meant that we were going further than we had ever gone before. As I realise that this may be more than a holiday, panic also strikes as I also realise what was at stake.

We get out of the taxi, and I hold my little brother's hand. My mum was holding my sisters' hand and our black plastic bag, containing everything we owned. I followed my mum to the ticket booth. As we approached the clear Perspex window, I saw a lady with grey hair in a green uniform. I wondered how many other people that she had served, were also running away from something or to something. Imagine if she only knew what a pivotal role, she may have played in so many people's lives. As the lady began to speak to my mum, I watched the station entrance, wishing she would hurry up. The lady asked my mum 'where to?' The lady and I stared at my mum waiting for the answer, she replied 'anywhere,' whichever is the first coach that is leaving, we will have tickets for that.' The lady said that a coach was leaving in five minutes, it was going to a faraway city that I had never heard of before.

We purchased our tickets and made our way quickly to the stand. As we got there, the coach was firing up its engine, ready to depart. We safely climbed on board and sat down. I had a window seat with my brother sitting on my lap. Mum sat next to me with my sister.

There was still a minute or so to go. I started to feel sick. My life had been lived, walking on the sharpest pieces of broken glass, intricately embedded in the thinnest ice. I was gradually progressing one day at a time just by being alive.

This day felt like it was about to be the final stretch. Would we make it across, or would the ice finally crack and consume us? I could not remove my eyes from the station entrance. It sounds overly dramatic to think that at any time, he could come running through that gate and stop us from leaving, but it was not. Our lives mimicked that of a movie. Things that were done to us in real life would usually only exist in the imaginations of the best psychological writers. It was not far-fetched to expect him, the villain, to arrive at the very last minute.

The only real difference separating our lives and that of a film was that in movies, good prevailed, but that was not the case in real life.

The coach doors closed, and the bus dropped its body down as the driver removed the hand brake. The cocktail of suspense, fear, and excitement had rendered my body inactive. The wheels of the coach began to turn. We were no longer walking on ice; we were about to make it to the other side.

As the coach gently pulled out of the station, I wanted to shout, 'hurry up!' I knew he could still appear as if out of nowhere and jump in front of the bus, demanding we get off. I was looking for him because that was how it always transpired, whether it be three weeks or three hours, we left, and he found us.

We were out of the station and on the road. As we drove through the city centre, only daring to glance out of the window, we still did not feel that we could afford to exhale; not yet he was ingenious.

As the wheels spun us out of the city centre, we cried tears, shared silent smiles, and exchanged looks of disbelief. The journey took five hours but to be honest. I could have stayed on that coach forever. I was snuggled up to my mum, my angel, with my siblings safe.

NEW LANDS

We arrived in our new city with our plastic bag of possessions like hopeful pioneers fresh off a boat. During the late nineties, domestic violence started getting traction; it was now acknowledged as needing both resources and awareness. Certain cities had new helplines funded, for the thousands of calls they now received every day. We were not arriving in our new town in the late nineties.

There were no helplines yet, so my mum did the only thing she knew and called the police. The police told her to stay where she was and that someone would call her back shortly. After ten long minutes, a women's refuge rang the phone box back, they spoke to my mum and told her to give them our exact whereabouts, and they would send a taxi for us.

I was so happy. This escape felt real. We settled down quickly, we were no strangers to women's refuges. I enjoyed them, the communal living, the mix of diverse types of women in them, and the kids. I did not know what my mother had told them, and I did not bother asking.

One day, the house manager called my mum into the office for a talk. I hung around outside the door, leaning in, while stroking the cold wall with my shoulder. I listened as best as I could, but I could only make out muffled voices. It sounded serious from the tones and the long pauses. Unexpectedly, a word managed to break through. It travelled, carried by air, and bounced off the drums in my ears. It was a word I did not want to hear; someone said 'police.'

I panicked on hearing this. Had my dad somehow managed to get the police to track us down to a whole different city? Surely not? Based on his past capabilities to manipulate people, I had to admit that yes, it was possible.

The door opened, and my mother appeared. My mum did not seem surprised to see me there. She ushered me to come in. The lady behind the desk looked at me with great sympathy. The lady went on to explain to me what she had just explained to my mum.

I was in pieces, my soul was back at the side of me, and my heart was now on the floor. The refuge manager told me that she had received a call from the local police in our city of origin. The police had tracked my family and me down because they needed to talk to us. They wanted to speak to us because my dad had done something terrible to two random young women. My dad was currently locked up in jail.

HE KNEW IT

I could not help but smile. I put myself back together, and my thoughts turned to the young women who were now entangled in our roots. They told me the few details that they had, and I could put together the rest. When I say the rest, I mean the frames prior to him cementing his fate.

I had a picture of what may have transpired because we are not just the bodies we carry around. We are souls, or energy or spirit. Whatever you want to call it, that is us. That energy is all-knowing and all-seeing.

If we can be still and quiet enough, that knowing becomes a reliable source of information.

No matter who you are, you can tap into this intelligence. Sadly, we spend a substantial portion of our lives living contrary to this intelligence. We have been conditioned to not only distrust others, but more importantly, ourselves. In its simplest form, we see it materialise in our intuition. If you can learn to be mindful and believe in yourself, you can live in this intuition. This is the merging of our minds with our souls.

I could feel the scene as I closed my eyes. My dad had come home from the betting shop and performed his usual tasks. We were not there, and that was fine; we were probably out buying groceries. After an hour and a half, he started getting restless. He poured himself a brandy and sat back down. He looked at his watch, and it was past teatime. Panic slowly started to creep in, flowing from the tips of his fingers and toes, filling his body with uncertainty. It is night-time now. He only realises how much time had passed, when he looked at the empty brandy bottle that is perched on the arm of his chair, informatively casting an empty shadow.

'Where is she? She would never dare wander off for this amount of extended time and not take care of his meal. He started to admit to his fear. He went to look in the wardrobe and saw that our clothes were still there. His chest dropped slightly, and he relaxed a little. He then went to the bathroom just to double-check, but then saw that our toothbrushes were gone.

As he looked in the mirror and rested his strong hands on the white porcelain sink, he knew we were gone. He also knew that we were gone for good. In the end, he has lost. He started to get that defeated feeling, the feeling of sinking and drowning. As he realised, he has completely lost control, he heavily slumps down to sit on the floor with his back against the bath. Thoughts swirl, slowly turning and churning into feelings.

He cannot stabilise, the thoughts disappeared and left behind anger that words cannot represent. He picks himself up off the floor and punches the mirror. Someone was going to pay, and they do. He walked out of the front door, seething and hungry for a catch.

He turned left and walked up the five steps to our neighbours' door. Two young women live there alone, they were students. He knocked on the door. His fake smile hid the fire. A girl answered. He asked her if she had seen his wife and kids. She is apprehensive and replied, 'sorry, no.' As he stared, probing her face, he remembered how the girl resembles his wife. The girl was red-haired with pale skin, like a beautiful porcelain doll.

He pushed through the door, covered her mouth with his hand, and locked the door behind himself. He kidnapped and assaulted the two women in their own home. It was forty-eight hours before her family came knocking and alerted the police.

His intuition told him that we were gone, gone. Otherwise, he would have never risked jail like that. He was intelligent, calculated, and manipulative, never threatening his own persona.

It was a lot to take in. The lady looked at me, and I looked at mum. I knew what was coming. The lady said that she needed to ask me an extremely sensitive question. Was I ok with that? I said, 'sure.' She went to the door and invited another lady in, she was called Margret, and she was to be my social worker for the next twelve months.

Once Margret was seated, the refuge manager asked me if my dad had ever laid his hands on me other than the beatings. I felt like I was playing visual ping pong, batting glances from the manager to my mum, the social worker, and back to rest on my mum's face. She looked deep into me and said, "don't worry," she knew what I was thinking. I was thinking how much this was going to hurt her, and she had hurt enough. My mum continued to question me with her eyes. I said yes.

Having kids, myself, I could not even begin to understand, how her heart would have broken on hearing my response. The social worker took over and asked me very childlike if he had touched me with certain things in certain places. I said 'yes.' I did not need the softly, softly approach; I had been learning about sex for seven years. The social worker said that I might have to make a video statement for court for him to be punished for this. I was then told by the social worker that I would need to go to a special clinic straight away to have a test. The test would determine if my hymen were still intact. I already knew the answer. I had lost my virginity years ago.

I do not ask much from this world, but I do wish with all my heart, that I can see the day that my mother forgives herself for the things that she did not know.

I have always lived with the notion that I have to turn my childhood experience on its head and make it count. I realised now that you do not have to find meaning in the actual trauma. The traumas inflicted on us were not our 'lessons,' we are merely collateral damage in someone else's story. Although we do not have to find meaning in the trauma inflicted by someone else, there is something precious to be gained because of it. Growth lies in the aftermath of the trauma. To access this growth, I had to be aware that I was on a journey and comfortable in understanding that this journey may span the rest of my life.

Finding peace within, allowing ourselves to travel through the pain and messiness, is what transmutes the trauma into something beautiful. It is no longer the trauma that is us but the things we have learned following it. We can pass onto others to help them. We become the 'get ups,' not the fall.

The resilience and strength I have gained during the rollercoaster ride of finding peace are matched by no other experience. I cannot change the past, but I have changed my projected future.

I would like to say that we lived happily ever after, but it was not all happy. Healing is not always pretty. When things get tough, I remember at least I am free, I am safe, I am loved, and I am understood.

DRIPPED IN SUNSHINE

Our first house in our new freedom was beautiful. Our home was deep in the belly of an inner-city council estate. In this house on the bare wooden floors, with little to no furniture, I learned how to be a woman. I watch my mother flourish. I saw her breakthrough her fears, taking a seat in her newfound independence.

I never saw any aftereffects of the trauma that my mum had endured. Whatever pain she was going through during these early days, she kept to herself. She was the calm and patient mother that my teen daughter had needed me to be. I do not know if she consciously kept her pain from me or if I was too self-absorbed, enjoying being a teenager.

I watched her build things. I watched her make things. I watched her paint walls, plaster, and wallpaper. I watched her slowly find the money to furnish our house. I watched her find the confidence to go to work. I watched as her spirit danced while she cleaned the house. Every day seemed like summer as the sun shone in through our windows and bathed her in light.

I would watch the local teenagers spending time together on the street quietly from behind my bedroom net curtain. I was too shy to make friends. One day while hidden behind my lace net curtain watching, I saw one of the boys walking toward my house. What is he doing? Is he coming to knock on my door? Butterflies erupted within me.

The boy bent down and picked something up off the ground; it was a small stone. He threw the rock at my window. I froze. Can he see me? He threw another little stone; I move the curtain back and open my window. 'Yes,' I said. Simply with a smile, he said, 'come out.'

I became part of a group of teen boys and girls that lived on and around the estate. I had so much fun. I felt that this must be what I had wished for all those times something was missing. We were free, but before that day, I was alone.

My only concerns in life at this stage were getting home from school as fast as possible to hang out with my friends. The freedom that I was beginning to accept was uncontrollable in me. I was a teenager who felt like she had already lived many lives.

The skills that I had learned to survive were now being executed on my mum. I wanted to exercise my freedom to its fullest. I did not think that I should have things like curfews and rules, those were for kids, and I did not have the pleasure of having lived a child's life.

I did not understand that she was trying her best to protect me. She was trying to protect me from myself. A sharp and intuitive mind could get me far, but my lack of experience in the outside world could have easily been my downfall. At fifteen, my girlfriends and I would drink alcohol and hang out at the park. We would talk, dance and sing. We had each other's back. I had one or two steady boyfriends during this time (steady meaning three months at that age), nothing serious.

We would occasionally smoke weed if we had the money, and we would go to house parties on the estate. Our parents never worried where we were on the estate because everyone knew each other and trusted each other.

I would sometimes play with my younger siblings, and the younger kids next door who were from a children's home. Mum and my social worker had managed to get me into a great school that was far away. I did not mind. I still enjoyed learning and was a good student. I made good friends there.

I felt like a part of the community. I started consensual sexual activity just before I was sixteen. Around the same time, I started going out to the big club nights. I also started recreationally experimenting with drugs. I tried the drug LSD (trips) and went to big warehouse parties where I danced in bliss until the sun came up.

When I danced on these nights, I felt free. I was able, for four hours, to reclaim my body as my own. The LSD helped me detach from all that had made me. It gave me a certain clarity that there was more to life. I was happy during my years of being a teen. I had more freedom than ever and was constantly pushing for more. Despite this, a sense of being trapped inside myself remained. I was now outwardly free, but chains held my authenticity securely inside of me.

The invisible chains were there to remind me that there was evil in the world and people could not be trusted. The chains reminded me that I was constantly being judged. My dad's living ghost haunted me. When I danced on these nights, I could be the real me, me without the baggage, the me that was confident and would put the world to rights. I talked to strangers for hours on end, and I was able to not only share my pain but listen to the pain of others.

When I threw my arms up in ecstasy, darkness, and colour mixed in the air to create an energetic rain that drenched me in bliss, I would spin around and around, smiling up at the grey ceiling. Those nights were drug-fuelled, yes, but they were once a month at most. I do not wish to defend the use. It enabled me to feel a love and a connection to the world that my counsellor had not helped me to know.

I am not condoning random and illegal drug use; however, scientific research is starting to emerge on the positive effects of controlled psychedelic use on trauma and addiction, the results look promising. If therapies are effective, it should not be a matter concerning public opinion. Societies' opinions change from one day to the next and are therefore unreliable.

People are changing, and the way we respond to trauma is also changing

CEMENTING THE SITUATION

The separation between my mum and me had already happened by the time I was sixteen. This time, the separation was not because of a locked door or an unspoken rule but a natural separation. I was pulling away because I was becoming an adult. It is interesting how as teens, we subconsciously know what is to come. We understand that the time is coming to stand on our own. Unfortunately, our society does not encourage the understanding of this transition.

As a teen, you act subconsciously in a way that drives wedges between you and your family. You do things that cause chaos and conflict because it is the only way we know to create more space between us. Really, we are scared and do not want that space, but society tells us we must become fully functioning adults.

Parents are encouraged to cut the apron strings, and we are told to grow up. The separation was further extended as my mum met someone she fell deeply in love with. I was on guard, but I liked him. Although he was younger than my mum, he had a good heart and added strength in numbers for her.

He was a bright and intuitive man. Because of this, I could not pull the usual stuff that I did to my mum to manipulate her. By sixteen, all I was concerned with was settling down with someone. I wanted my own family to correct the unhappiness of my own childhood experience. My mum was an angel, and she showed me how an independent woman carried herself. She taught me that hurt people do not always have to hurt people. She could not, however, teach me that with which she had not yet learned herself.

I was not taught that there were other pathways in life, I was not taught that the love I was searching for could be found within myself, I was not taught that being a parent and trying to live with trauma is one of the hardest things you can ever go through. I was not taught to find myself and heal before doing anything else. All I knew was that I should finish school as best as possible, go to college or get a job and then make a home and family. Up until the last year of school, I was an A+ student with fantastic potential. As the end drew near, my focus dwindled into nothing. I felt like it was not fair.

I had only had two years being a teen, and now I was supposed to move on to adult life. I pushed school to the side. I stopped going to classes and instead did the things I enjoyed. By the time my exams came and went, I left school with the basics only. No one saw it coming; I had always done so well academically, so it was no wonder everyone expected I would continue to do so. They did not notice me slowly slipping. I left school and signed up for college to study psychology.

Just before my sixteenth birthday, months after finishing high school, I found myself at my favourite place to dance. I was at a big warehouse club night that was close to where I lived. I was dancing away with my friends when I started to feel a little dizzy. I sat down on the floor with my back against the concrete cooling wall. I began to feel better and became aware of someone staring at the side of me. I turned my head to the side and saw a boy staring at me. He said 'hello,' and I said 'hi.' He then looked me up and down and told me that I would be leaving with him.

I laughed at his apparent cheek, considerable confidence, and proceeded on with my night.

I ignored him for the rest of the night because he was not my type, and I was not a fan of his persistence. He eventually wore me down with his continued 'dance stalking,' and I gave in and danced with him. We talked, and we smoked cigarettes, and then we danced some more. I agreed to get a lift home with him and his friends. We exchanged home numbers, and that was it. I told him I was about to turn eighteen, but really, I was about to turn sixteen.

Little did I know during that ride home how influential this boy would be in my life.

CHAPTER THREE

✥

The Loop

LOVE THE DRUG

He was older than me by two years, he was eighteen, and I was sixteen. At sixteen, eighteen was a lifetime more of experience. He drove and had a car, which was super impressive for a sixteen-year-old girl. He had already had a serious two-year-long relationship (which was likened to marriage at our age). I felt like he was very experienced in both life and love. In the beginning, I was not attracted to him. The night we met; my friend had pulled me away from him. He was big and imposing, and he was obvious.

We met up in the city, and he took me out for drinks or food. I enjoyed it. I felt grown-up and liked how special I was being treated. I loved that when we went out to clubs, bars, or restaurants, you could tell that he was proud to have me on his arm. I had never been made to feel worthy by anyone other than my mum.

I ended up falling for him because of his confidence in himself, he did not care about what anyone thought about him, and I aspired to be the same. While dating, we would go places where he did not belong culturally, not to be an antagonist, but just because he enjoyed that culture. We would have the best time. He walked the earth like he was ten men rolled into one, and that made me feel safe.

I fell for the idea of not only him but his family. You would not think it on meeting him because he acted the opposite, but he came from a sleepy, upper-middle-class village. For an unknown reason, he wanted to be part of, and resonated with urban inner-city life. I found it interesting to meet someone that still had a traditional family setup.

I fell in love with the idea of his family because it was something I had never had. I loved their traditional Sunday dinners with all the generations of the family sitting around the dining table. He was from a conventional background but appreciated urban life.

My first and only addiction was the version of love that I was receiving from him. I very quickly became dependant. I would sit with his perfect nuclear middle-class family for Sunday dinners and admire their closeness. The separation between myself and my family slowly started to feel even bigger. The assimilation into his life was almost seamless. I was spending more time in his world, while drifting further away from mine.

The happy ever after now seemed like a possibility, he worked, and I would soon be working. He was eager to get a mortgage as quickly as possible. There was a future developing of which I had only ever dreamed. We could be a mum and dad together, with a house, three happy kids, with our extended family sitting around a large dining table every weekend. Bliss.

His life felt so far away from my past that I clung to it for dear life. The relationship was all good for the first year. We dated, we drank, we danced, and we laughed. Things slowly started to change. We would go out clubbing, and he would end up in fights with bouncers or people that seemed weaker than him. I would be annoyed that he ruined the night. We would come home, and I would question his motives and his actions, and then we would argue.

Eventually, the arguments would turn to mental abuse. The mental abuse from my partner started with repetitive abandonment. The abandonment started at my partner's parents' home. We would argue in the middle of the night, and I would be distraught.

He would tell me to get out of his room which I would refuse to do because his mum used to sit up late. I did not particularly want to sit with her in tears. He would eventually throw me out of his room, and his mum would come to get me and take me downstairs. After a while, he would go as far as throwing me out of his mum's house.

He once dragged me to his front doorstep half-naked and threw my clothes at me. I did not drive, and he lived in a country village, miles away from where I lived. Other times he would send me home and ignore me for days on end. I would be at home curled up in the foetal position crying and stressed, wishing my head would just explode. I would stay like this until he eventually contacted me. There would be no apology, just a brushing of problems under the carpet. I did not care; I just wanted to be back at his, where my dreams of my happy ever after were safe.

I was around eighteen at this point. At eighteen, I got an apprenticeship in a busy hairdressing shop in a vibrant student area. I met an amazing group of girls, which was good because, at that point, I had none left of my own. I had devoted two years to him and my quest for a new life. I was entirely dependent on him. After an abandonment, I would go to work in tears, watching the reception phone, waiting for him to call. The pain of him leaving me felt so bad at times I did not want to continue living.

AN UNCONSCIOUS KNOWING

On my nineteenth birthday, my boyfriend and I went to a nightclub. Before we even got into the club, he had picked a fight with a bouncer. We ended up going straight home, arguing all the way. I was so angry, and we continued to argue in his bedroom. I was seated in an armchair only three feet across from him, he picked up a McDonald's tray that he used to have as a novelty and skimmed it across the room at my head. It caught the top of my lip, and it started pouring with blood. By this time in our relationship, I had told him the basics of my childhood; I had told him it was extremely violent. The fact that he could do this after knowing what I had already been through was a massive shock to me.

My younger self obviously did not see the red flags building up. Contemplating how this human being that I loved and loved me back could physically hurt me, traumatised me. I had thought I was safe, and I had thought that my dad was an extreme case of a human being. Now I was faced with the notion that violence may just be a norm, especially if love was involved. I cried hysterically; eventually, his mum came in and took me out of his room to calm me down.

The next day he abandoned me. Even though he had drawn his first blood, I needed him even more. There was no one else, so the abandonment felt one hundred times more painful. I wanted him to phone me and say he was coming to pick me up. I did not want to be at home, I wanted to be with him and work towards the future I deserved. The instances of violence slowly built up to a push, a shake, and a slap. I would cry in despair as my dreams faded from bright, vibrant images to heavy fog. He never felt bad for what he did. He believed that there was always a reason I caused the situation. Eventually, he was able to buy a house.

I was around twenty-two years old, when he brought the house, it was in his name only, even though I was working and paying half to everything. It was here in what was supposed to be the unfolding of my dream future that he really tried to break me. The mental and physical violence increased more as I tried to forge a life outside of the home. I was still completing my apprenticeship, but I had realised that there really was no long-term future in the trade for me, and I wanted more. Hairdressing had done me well, but it was not my passion. I decided to finish the apprenticeship anyway because I knew that having a trade was still a valuable skill to have.

A SEED IS SOWN

Before leaving my trade, after considering my next move, I decided that I would go to university. This was the first of my wild dreams; no one in my family had gone to university. Procrastination about leaving my trade was taken away from me, I was made redundant. Another job was found quickly, as I was living away from home and had to support myself. The job was in a supermarket. While working in the supermarket I figured out my path to university. Three months into the job, I found out I was pregnant.

It was a strange time. The work was hard in the supermarket. It was the kind of business that really made you work for your wage. I would be cleaning the car park at five in the morning, finding leftover drug appliances.

Despite the hard physical work and the job of having and hiding my morning sickness, I felt a sense of grace. I felt special. I was carrying a child. The beautiful job of growing this child had been bestowed upon me.

The violence calmed down and was replaced with more psychological abuse. There were happy times in between the abuse, a first scan, the first shopping trip for baby clothes, and decorating the room. Unfortunately, these times did not last. The minute I wanted a say in something or disagreed with a decision, he would pull rank. He had conditioned me over the years to believe that I had nothing and knew nothing. Anything that I did know he knew better. The conditioning he gave me was encapsulated in a phrase he used often when describing me, he called me 'damaged goods.

My partner succeeded in making me look back at my life, particularly the way my mum had argued back with my dad. I would compare to my own behaviour arguing and fighting back. For a minute, I believed he could be right, it was our fault. I know now he was gaslighting me and had done for years. He loved in the early days to play 'urban' and 'disadvantaged,' which is one of the reasons I fell for him. I felt like he understood and celebrated the diverse cultures and was sensitive to the plight of those in lower socio-economic backgrounds.

This understanding seemed to now disappear. If you were from that type of background like I was and questioned him, he would reveal another persona, middle class and well to do. He broke me repeatedly, throughout the relationship, but when I look back, I do not see myself as a victim. I always fought back. I always defended myself and my family.

When I found out I was pregnant, a meeting was arranged with my mum to tell her. After delivering the news of the pregnancy to my mum she asked me what I was going to do. I responded I was going to have a baby. At this response, her face fell into a soft sadness. We talked, and I acknowledged the state of the relationship. Still, I also realised that the violence had died down and that I believed one thing to be true of him and that this child would be his world, regardless of whether we were together or not.

A NEW STRENGTH

The birth of my daughter was less than ideal. An induction was planned as the pregnancy had already gone fourteen days over. The nurse gave me a tablet that was supposed to take twenty-four hours to take effect. Twenty-four hours was not the case for me. Within the hour, I was spiralling anxiously into full-blown labour. My partner and mother had been sent home under the expectation that labour would not start for a while.

Just as my partner and my mum returned, I was rushed into a cold, sterile, grey theatre. The contractions were horrendous, only three hours into the labour, and I had given up. I had no energy left to give; it was only after I heard the midwife proclaim that they would have to cut me that I found the strength to give one last almighty push. And there she was. We had not known what sex the baby was, as during the previous scans, she had crossed her legs. The entire world seemed different suddenly.

The previously lifeless delivery room now was sun-drenched. I felt true happiness and freedom. With my daughter lying on my beating heart, I felt the freedom of love. I would no longer be bound by how much someone loves me, or how I compare to the rest of the world as a human being. I did not care about anything anymore, just her. That night, she triggered a spark in me. The life I had been living was no longer good enough. The birth of my daughter brought both darkness and light.

On the one hand, I would feel this overwhelming love and hope for the world, but on the other hand, I felt this immeasurable pressure weighing deep down on my soul. This tiny human was mine to raise. She was mine to keep safe. The conditions of her childhood and the decisions I made could affect her whole adult life. The realisation of this responsibility rattled my core. The pressure was on. That same pressure also gave birth to a strength I never knew I had.

By the time she was a couple of months old, the violence had started again, it was not regular, but it was still there. The psychological bullying never really left. If anything, it got worse. My partner had not thought it appropriate to be physically violent to a pregnant woman, a boundary my dad never had. I do not know if the bullying got worse after the birth, or my post-partum hormones made it feel worse. I took cover in the responsibility of my daughter, feeding her at my breast, holding her, and bathing her. I would lay next to her for hours on end, just watching her breathe.

When my daughter was around five months old, I made the mental decision to really start to plan how I was going to be able to support us both on my own. The house we lived in was his, and he had made it so that he was the only one that had surplus finances to save. I told him that I would go to college to do an access course that would then take me to university to do a Social Work Degree. He was OK with this as it meant that he could keep even more of his to himself if I were earning more. I started going to college two days a week. His mother and father would babysit our daughter while I was there. My studies during my access course really changed my life forever. I studied sociology, psychology, and social work. Sociology really opened my eyes to how the different structures in society work and how those structures came to be.

I learned that little in this world was how it was by chance. I knew that inequalities, sexism, and racism were systematic and perpetuated over centuries to maintain a structure. On a deeper level, I learned that if systems like sexism could be put in place, then on a personal level, they could be removed. One of the biggest triggers for him and me was the gender struggles within the relationship. He came from a traditional white, middle class, army family. He believed that I should do everything in the home even when I was working equal hours. I fought against this and demanded, as best I could, equality.

A BOX OF MEN

When reflecting on the evolution of males, it is easy to see that throwing them all in the box marked 'men' had just as many negative consequences, as putting all females into the box labelled 'Women.' While women were being shushed, degraded, and reduced to thinking their only aspirations in life should be to marry and reproduce. Men were being taught that the future of the human species rested on their 'strong' shoulders.

These boxes were not always in place. The authorities decided that having these boxes would be a more straightforward way of managing society. They did this not just with the male/female boxes, the rich/poor, the black/white, and of course the class boxes; that way, everyone knew their place. We have grown up in societies that, while seeming to become more progressive, are just creating more boxes. The more boxes, the less chance of people realising that we all bleed red. We are all in the same position, that is, unless you are a part of the 1%.

THE PROVIDER SYNDROME

In today's past and traditional cultures, boys would be groomed to be providers and protectors, like their fathers before them. Children do not always learn what you tell them, but they learn from what they see. The boy of the past was told he would provide for his blood family when they were old and provide for his own future family.

Not only was he verbally taught these things, but more importantly, it is what he saw. He saw his mum stay at home maintaining the house and children. He saw his sister encouraged to help mum with the female duties while he would help dad fix something. He saw that his dad was the boss, well respected, and sometimes even feared. Being a Man was very appealing to him.

Fast forward to the nineties, things started to change for those sons and their mothers. Specific practices that had walked hand in hand with men's dominance were becoming less acceptable. Domestic violence was one of them. With increased support available and police policies taking it more seriously, women were able to leave abusive marriages. This left a surge in single mothers. That boy was now predominantly raised by his mother. This was great subconsciously for his sister because she now had a role model in her mother. She saw that it was not ok to accept being treated in a certain way.

It was hard for the son because he had grown with dad as boss with him next in line for the throne. Now he had to get used to this newly confident, independent version of his mother and sister. They, without realising it, felt a surge of female power. He may even have to deal with a new male figure in the home. He struggles to deal with this. He feels that he should be the head of the household now. The boy is told that he is a child and does not have the right to an opinion. His mother was currently working, she is their provider, and she deserved respect.

The son then goes into adult life, still demanding the respect he saw his father get as my first partner did. The respect of his birth right just for being a man. The problem is that he now lives in a world that is not like that of his fathers. Now his world is becoming full of women finding their personal power, women asking questions, and women realising there is another way that does not involve them being classed as a weaker sex.

The man subconsciously looks to find the old school relationship his mother and father had in terms of power. Funnily enough, what does the universe send him? Strong woman after strong woman. At first, he finds it an attraction that they are strong. After already falling for them, he remembers the goal of finding a submissive woman who will be a good wife and mother.

The strong or potentially strong woman (I classed my younger self as potentially strong) is not an easy relationship. She demands equality even if she is not sure what that is. All she may know is that there is a sometimes-invisible expectation of her to be a certain way, and she is not exactly sure why. She asked, why I should do that? Why is that ok for you and not for me?

Although he remembers his goals, it is too late because he has already fallen for her. So, what does he do? He tries to break her strength. He succeeds after some time, but she will inevitably rise again, to go through the cycle a few times more until she decides to leave him. He does not know how to live in the new world because no one ever explained it to him. His dad never gave him the skills he needed to live in the current world because he never knew it was coming himself. It had been the same for centuries. Him, his dad and his grandad, and his great grandad all maintained the throne.

WHO DO I THINK I AM?

My daughter's father had gotten away with treating me as an unequal human being for a long time. He was able to achieve this because he controlled the money. Today they call this financial abuse.

At this point, he had everything. As a bonus, he had managed to condition me consciously and subconsciously, to believe that I was a less worthy human being. It was not just his grip on my mind that was strong, but I secretly held on too. Deep down, I was still living in the false hope that we could have a 'typical' happy conclusion.

When my daughter came along, my priorities changed. It was all about her. He felt how deep my love was for her, and he suspected that this love was stirring a new strength in me.

College was hope for my daughter and me. It promised stability and independence. The learning that I encountered at college, seven years after finishing school as a mother of one, was a completely unique experience. It was an empowering experience; I chose it, and I embraced every bit of it.

I had always asked questions. In my early years, the questions fluttered around my unfortunate incarnation. As a child, I obviously wondered why only some people had pain, while some did not. My early age did not deter me from asking questions that I now understand to be of a philosophical nature. As an adult, the focus of my questions allowed a much broader focus. I was more concerned with the bigger picture of society and life.

I passed my college course, and I applied for university. Shockingly to me, I was accepted into university. I was going to be the first in my family to continue to higher education. I was supposed to be enrolled in a Social Work degree, but on the first day, I found out that I was registered for the wrong course. I was registered for Sociology. There are no mistakes. Although I was not yet consciously walking my spiritual journey, I did not question the error. I knew that if I did not like it, I would more than likely change courses later. I was happy that I had even made it to university.

I still do not know how I passed my access course, authored essays, and took exams while in a relationship with a partner who employed psychological warfare. I went ahead and started my Sociology Degree and loved every minute of it. I put my daughter into childcare, and despite how hard things were at home, I continued slowly, one foot in front of the other.

I knew that the relationship was drawing to its end, and I would have to be ready. I became more confident as a mother and as myself. I always had the strength ingrained deep within me; I just had to dig deep to realise it. I was starting to feel a sense of pride in being female. In my mind, the narrative was changing. I was moving from female subordinate to female empowered.

I made inspiring new female friends in university; they were mature students like me. We would spend lunchtimes putting the world to rights and joining dots. The more I learned, the more I was exposed to different people, the less respect I had for him and his ways.

As my confidence grew, so did the violence at home. Towards the end of the first year of my degree, the abuse was reaching a crescendo. He had crossed so many lines, and yet every time he did, I was still surprised. He knew how hard I was working, trying to get through my first year of university while at the same time trying to be the best mum I could be. He knew what I had already endured and still hurt me.

I fought back every chance I had. I was not a scared child anymore. Fighting back made the violence worse; I suspected that he preferred it that way. I would scream and cry at him during these times. It was never about the event. I was accustomed to them; my cries and screams were a release of frustration. Life was still unfair. How could he relish in the dismantling of my soul, knowing the pain that already lived there? How could I ever trust again?

I barely made it onto the second year of my degree. One night during the summer holidays before the start of my second year, I was getting ready to go out with my girlfriends. My daughter was two and a half years old at the time. He started making comments, pulling on straws. He was not happy. The more I ignored him, the more his anger grew. I was not going to let him ruin the night.

His voice changed with his temper building. I could hear the quickening of his breaths. I needed to leave. I watched myself in the mirror as I finished my make-up. He was behind me. The rage slowly released as he spat insults through his barred teeth. I wondered how long I could remain calm.

I turned around to look him in his eyes; maybe I could calm him. Probably not. I could not win, ignore him, anger him, or argue back. He suddenly grabbed my shoulders and started violently shaking me. The next thing I knew was that I was on the floor and confused.

I lifted my hand up to my forehead. I felt a massive bubble, I was disorientated, but I slowly got up and looked in the mirror. On my head was what looked like a huge blood blister that almost covered my forehead.

I started to panic. He headbutted me so hard I hit the ground and blacked out. As I came around, he scoffed at me in my alarm. With an emotionless face, he declared that I should get to the hospital.

My daughter was crying and stood up in her crib. I looked at her and knew this was it. I still loved him, but this was my time to choose, so I did. I called my mum, and her boyfriend to come and pick us up. I packed a black bag of clothes as my mother had done with us, and we left.

CHAPTER FOUR

The Beginning

OUR FIRST HOME

We arrived at the beginning of August. My mum's house was a two-bedroom house with my brother occupying one and her the other. My daughter and I were crammed into my mums' room with her. I did not care. I was grateful to have her there while I spent weeks doing nothing but crying. I stayed in bed, I did not eat, and I felt devastated.

I knew that this was authentic, all the hopes, and dreams of giving my daughter a traditional family setup had dramatically been swept away. After weeks of grieving the death of my relationship, I received notification that I passed my first year of university, and I was able to continue to the second year. It was great news. I passed, albeit narrowly.

Towards the end of the second week of August, I arose from my mums' bed, I dusted myself off, and I got ready to fight for us.

By the first week in September, just before university commenced a new academic year, I had secured a part-time job at a major local supermarket. I worked weekends and one evening during the week. That same week I also secured me and my daughter's first home. Everything was falling into place. Our house was a simple, cosy house, and it became our haven. It felt uplifting to be independent. It felt good to not owe anyone anything and to not rely on anyone for our basic needs. I felt freedom in having the space to do the things I wanted to do. Simple things like hanging a piece of artwork gave me great comfort. The energy in our home was cheerful and full of gratitude. University was going well, and my friendships within the university were growing stronger. My daughters' father was consistent, and he started having her every weekend. This was helpful as I worked all weekends. My daughter enjoyed being with her dad and her dad's family and was secure in her routines.

The relationship between her father and me was still fragile. We would still argue but never in front of my daughter. He still tried to maintain any control, employing bullying whenever possible. The bitterness was now from a distance. Despite our passive-aggressive relationship, he proved to be a good dad, he loved her, and she loved him. I went through a period of going out at the weekends, I would go out with my university girlfriends, and we would dance our butts off. The house was so quiet without my daughter. I did not really know what else to do but to go out, dance and drink. Two years went by, and I had finished my first degree. I gained a Bachelor with Honours in Sociology & Cultural Studies.

By this time, my daughter was five years old and was already at a small school. Life was a struggle for me. I had little money as a student and single parent; her dad had tried to use finances to exercise his control. He had accused me of using the money he would give for all kinds of outlandish things.

In the end, I had told him to just put the money he would contribute into her schooling. That way, he could not accuse me of spending his money. We enrolled her in a small school, and she quickly started showing signs of being more 'with it' than most adults. I did not drive, I had tried and failed, it was an expensive test to fail. I think that because I really needed it, the pressure stopped me from passing. My days were spent rushing from school to university, to work, to home, on one bus to the next. The dark winter nights were the hardest, picking her up from school and then sitting at the bus stop, cold and sometimes wet, watching all her friends drive past, warm and cosy in their cars. It would take us hours to get home. I could have sent her to a closer school, but this school gave her a far better start. I would do whatever it took. My daughter, of course, never complained. We would turn our travels into adventures, we were a little team, and if we were together, all was well.

One night during my daughter's fifth year of life, while tucking her into bed, I declared that 'one day we would live by a beach.' I wanted her to dream past the confines of walls or places. I told her that we would have to wait until she was eighteen. She asked me, why we would have to wait? I told her that it was because her dad loved her very much. He would never let me take her to a different country. I was astonished at my daughter's understanding when she replied, 'what's the point in that? I will not be a kid by then' She made complete sense. This small response from this little girl would be the glitch in my limited thinking. This small question would be the driving force for big plans.

After I finished my initial degree, I decided to take a year out and work. I gained a position at a chiropractor as a receptionist/x-ray developer. I had to make decisions about what I was going to do next. I knew my degree alone would not provide me with a stable career or income. I decided to do a teaching postgraduate specializing in English and found a job in a chiropractor in the meantime. I did not want to do primary teaching, and I did not want to be a high school teacher. I wanted to do sixteen plus education, which also included college students and adults. My reasoning behind this was that I had thoroughly enjoyed studying as a mature student. I wanted to be that person, like my teacher on my access course, that gave me the adult hope, that it was not too late. That hope I was given provided me with confidence that followed me to my postgraduate.

I wanted to help people. I started to see a picture of myself standing on a podium speaking. This picture came from nowhere and seemed outlandish at the time, just like my decision to pursue teaching as a career.

It was ridiculous because I was super shy and hated public speaking. Despite this, I thoroughly enjoyed the teaching course, and I understood why I needed it. It taught me one thing that I will never forget. The teaching course taught me how to overcome my fear of talking in front of other people.

During the course, I did practice lessons in front of my peers. Many of whom already had teaching experience and were many years my seniors. The course taught me that when you really had to do something that was so far out of your comfort zone that you felt you could faint, the only way forward was in honesty and in surrender.

When I stood up in front of my peers, I did so in honesty. I did not try and pretend to be perfect or know it all. I allowed the mistakes. I let go of trying to guess what the judgements of my peers were going to be or what they were thinking. I was able to gain the skills that I would use to teach challenging behaviour teens for the next few years.

ASK AND IT IS GIVEN

One weekend in December, we had massive amounts of snow. It was beautiful, white-topped roofs and warm glowing fires. My daughter had been at her fathers for the weekend, but because he was countryside based, he had ended up being snowed in. He was not able to bring her back on time. I was invited by my ex-colleagues to come to the local pub. I usually declined a Sunday session at the pub; however, learning that my daughter was snowed in with her dad meant I was at a loss for something to do, so I agreed.

The pub was heaving when I got there; it was warm, and it was glowing. It was bustling with Christmas spirit, the music played, the drink flowed, and I had a wonderful time. After copious amounts of alcohol, I took it upon myself to invite half of the pub, all my ex-work colleagues, even the ones I did not know, to come back to my house for more drinks. There we were traipsing through the snow, in a group of twenty people, drunk and happy. It was around a fifteen-minute walk to get to my house.

When we got back to my house, and continued drinking, laughing, chatting, and dancing as the music blared. I was sitting and talking to someone when I heard another person mention a particular famous person's name. He was a lyrical poet, a conscious and intelligent musician. I could not believe that someone here was also aware of this musician. Even more shocking was that when I locked eyes with this person, I realized that I had worked with this person while at university.

He had well and truly slid under my radar. I started reading the book titled 'The Journey of Souls' by Michael Newton. After doing extensive research on the afterlife and people's description of 'the place in between lives,' he discovered that soul mates have an agreed-upon trigger that will ensure they recognize each other in each life. The trigger may be the dazzle of an earring that catches the other person's eye, or as in our case, it could be a word uttered at exactly the right point in space and time. I went over to him, and we started to talk. Before I knew it, we were in deep conversation about everything possible. By the end of the night, our fates were sealed.

The funny thing is that only three days prior to this night, after a short relationship with the usual project type man, who needed saving, I had proclaimed that I was ready for something different, a different type of man than what I was attracting. I had, in that statement, began to see my own self-worth. I knew this relationship was going to be of significance as it felt so different. It felt different in that it did not feel like a fairy tale, at least not in the way we have been conditioned to perceive one. It did not start with the fake, over the top fairy tale feelings, the overpowering excitement as the prospect of a new chase, a new love addiction, begins. Do not be mistaken, we fell very much in love, but it was a calm and knowing love.

We had the arbitrary honeymoon period, but it soon moved into something else. It turned into a partnership. When the honeymoon period dissipated, it not only revealed a real partnership but feelings that were greater than any 'love' any man had given me. The feeling was confidence, confidence that no question marks were hanging over us, over me. There was no question mark over whether I was good enough, whether he would be able to deal with my demons or whether he could respect me enough, to be honest. I knew that I had been blessed with my life partner, the yang to my Ying. I went from being just me to a team.

I quickly knew in my heart that we would always move forward as a team, never opposed and never through ego. The love was committed and respectful. The confidence gave birth to action, and two years later, I gave birth to a beautiful baby boy.

My daughter adored him; she now had a real-life doll that she could look after. My daughter's dad struggled with me having another child, he never said as such, but I knew so. Even though we had been separated for years, it signified the ultimate end. When you have kids with someone there, that is until someone marries or has children with someone else. The feeling of having unwavering support was new to me. I felt like I could achieve anything. Instead of worrying about whether this relationship would work or not, wondering if he was faithful, my mind was free to create our future.

My partner had a family member who lived abroad with her kids. He would talk to her on Skype and show me pictures of her and her kid's life. We would look at where they live, where the kids went to school, and what they did for leisure. Over time I started to pay more attention. I noticed how happy they looked. I knew it was not all perfect; however, the life they were living resonated with me.

One evening while stalking his family online, I turned to my partner and said, 'shall we move there?' The words that came out of my mouth were a shock to both my partner and me. What was I thinking? I looked at my new baby boy and my daughter, and I thought about the life they too deserved to have. Where we lived was okay for us as adults, it was a vibrant student city, full of cultures from around the world, with epic nightlife, but it was not okay for our kids. Once you moved out of the centre, you would see that it was also plagued by homelessness, unemployment, low socioeconomics, and drugs.

I would never dream of letting my daughter play out in front of my house by herself. I could not allow her to ride her bike safely up and down the street. It was not okay that they would no longer feel like kids by their twelfth birthday, younger. The kids would have more of a childhood in the new country, crime rates were lower, and the general standard of living was higher. More than anything, it looked like you could make it be whatever you wanted. If you were rich, it could be expensive, you could live a high life. If you were not rich, you could still have a wonderful life. The new country offered free lifestyle activities, an abundance of natural places to explore. Beautiful beaches, clean parks, and beautiful forests to get lost in.

Urban life had been good to me, I had loved my city, but now with kids, it looked and felt different. When I thought about trying to go for this dream, I felt excited. A spark was ignited within me. I started to experience waves that ebbed and flowed, ebbs of excitement and flows of dread. I knew my daughter's dad would not let me take her, not easily anyway. No matter how much of a better life it was going to be for her, no matter how I welcomed him to visit, no matter how often she would come home to stay, none of it would be enough. I did not know if I had the fight in me required for this level of battle. I had been fighting my whole life. I started to feel stupid for even entertaining such an idea in my wildest dreams. At that point, my five-year-old daughter's question came back and sucker-punched me with the brightest clarity.

I remembered her asking me

"What is the point in waiting until I am eighteen?"

She was right. The images of her being able to be a child for longer were all I needed. My partner and I agreed to start looking into whether it was even possible. It was no easy feat to gain a visa into the new country. You had to jump serious hoops and have a skill in need. It would be one hell of a task, but we had hope, and hope can get you anywhere.

THE BATTLE BEGINS

The battle between my daughter's father and me over my need to emigrate was long and painful. I had to jump through hoops, not only to be awarded a visa for the new country but to be legally allowed to remove my daughter. What started off as an exciting dream quickly became a nightmare.

Her dad bullied me as best he could. He threatened my husband and me. I was called names, gaslighted, and convinced that I was an awful person. He did everything he could to make me feel like a deplorable human being.

When I entered this fight, I knew it would be painful, so I went into work mode. I had a job to do, and nothing was going to get in the way. On the odd occasion that I allowed myself to feel it, I felt so broken that I wondered if this was even worth it.

When the legal proceedings started, it was terrifying. I had never been to court before, and her dad had the upper hand as a court veteran.

I had never needed a solicitor; the whole thing was daunting. I made the court trips on my own as I did not want anyone else involved. I did a plethora of research; the whole dream was laid out in words and pictures on the pages I had started to put together.

I began to tackle the visa. I undertook tests and made an application to be sponsored by my chosen state. As I started to win the challenges, I became more optimistic. Each win, big or small, became another sign that what I felt deep in my heart was true.

After the first win, I was committed; the dream was now a real possibility. The profound sense of confirmed intuition did not mean I was released from experiencing lows. When flying high, I remained bound to the weight of my daughter's father, only going so high and then returning down.

I had my new husband, and I had hope, but there was still a large part of me that felt submissive to my daughters' father. I was still scared of him. I was not frightened of a physical threat from him but the old conditioning in me that he could still trigger.

I knew how he could change. I knew that he would do anything he could to stop us. There was no lie or low to which he would not stoop. I had tried to convince him that our daughter would have a better life. I told him he could come and stay with us anytime he wanted.

Towards the end of this battle, my husband saw me in unbelievably bad states of anxiety. I could no longer contain my feelings and fears. I had no choice but to wrap myself in a shield of Armour. That shield barely came down during those last months, even for him.

The first year we were together, I tried to be soft; I was ready for a different type of relationship. Unfortunately, as soon as we decided to seek a better life for our children, throwing myself into battle, I was quickly back in survival. My vulnerability was again buried away.

I used to call my husband my soul mate. I know today that he is not my soul mate but my twin flame. Only a twin flame would understand what I was a product of and what I had the potential to be.

This was despite how I treated him at times. The average male soul would not have stuck around after having his ego beaten to a moist pulp. I would say things to him like, 'I will never just be with you for the sake of having another person around.' I would declare that 'even if we emigrate and there is ever a time when you are not bringing something to the table, I will leave.' There was a constant reminder for him that I could do it all by myself. Somehow, he managed to hear past my words.

It was not until two years ago that I realised how I had treated him during the fight for a better life.

While he was driving us somewhere one day, I turned my head and stared at him; he smiled back at me lovingly and said, 'yes?' I told him I was sorry, and he replied, still smiling, 'sorry for what?'

We had already had, numerous happy years together since our battles. Because of this, he was genuinely confused about what I was sorry for. He may have forgotten, but I had not.

I told him that I was sorry if I had ever made him feel less than the man he was. He said, 'thank you,' but his eyes spoke of not needing that apology.

The person I was now able to be, was more than enough reward for him. At that point, he had spent the last eight years delivering consistency, loyalty, patience. His character gave me the security to slowly start to soften again. As I began to unwind, healing was able to be considered.

As the dream of emigrating became more of a reality, there was something I had to do. I wanted my children to have more family in the new country as they grew older and had their own kids. We decided to have one more child before leaving. I did not want to have our last child in the new country as my mother would be unable to be by my side. That was not an option for me.

Eight months before the big court case, I gave birth to a beautiful baby girl. I was absolutely in love yet again. I started to have visions of her and her brother, driving around our spacious open-plan house in their pretend cars in the new country. I held onto this vision for the next eight months.

THE FINAL SHOWDOWN

I had been consistently stepping closer to the edge, and any next step could be into mental deconstruction. My daughter's dad had tried everything, and at one point, such lies were told that child protection had become involved.

Child protection was not involved for long, but it was long enough to make me question this dream. Nothing in existence was worth losing your kids over. I was exhausted. I made it through to the end with the support of my best friend, my husband, and my family. On the day of the final court hearing, I felt I could stop breathing. I got myself dressed, I put on my makeup, and all the while knowing that this day would either bear the fruits of eighteen months' worth of fight or my hopes and dreams would for now be shattered. Today I would be shown if my intuition had served me well.

On the day of the court case, I struggled to hold it together. This battle was like none that I had fought before. The setting where the war would be fought alone, was debilitating. I had no trust in the institution that had let my mum and me down so many times.

I was still operating from my old systems. These systems were based on inadequacy, unworthiness, and low self-esteem. It did not matter to me that at this point, I had managed to graduate from university twice, marry an amazing man, and birth three beautiful kids. I still suffered from impostor syndrome.

Walking to the car, shaking, I ask myself, what am I doing? What made me think I could pull something of this magnitude off? Although I had been to court twice before, that was for formalities, to confirm things for the solicitors.

Today was the day that I had to plead my case, not to someone that knew me, knew my daughter, or even really cared. I had to plead my case to someone impartial and objective, and that brought with it fear.

I sat watching the minutes pass, patiently waiting to meet my barrister for the first time. I did not know how the law system worked, but I had been told by my solicitor, whom I had built a relationship with over the last two years, that he could only take me so far. The final showdown would need a barrister.

I remember looking around at the different micro-groups of people, and I found myself wondering what fate they were waiting to have confirmed or denied. Some looked like they were fighting for access to their child. Others looked like they were fighting for access to their own freedom. Other people looked like they were fighting to prove their innocence; families and groups of people looked anxious and scared.

This was the final episode for many of us in that waiting area. On occasions, this whole situation had threatened to evolve into something much more dangerous. Threats were made, and bluffs were called.

While deep in thought, a female voice says my name. I look up to see my barrister for the first time. God, the universe/the source of all things, whatever you want to call it, had sent me exactly what I needed.

As I looked up at her face and into her eyes, I felt a familiar feeling. I felt like I did when I watched the bird in the tree looking back at me as I peacefully fell to the ground from our balcony. I knew I was falling from the balcony, just like I knew I was falling sat waiting to go into court that day, but there was a feeling of safety. I knew that I was protected.

I was reminded by her very presence to have faith. I can only describe her as the epitome of power. This woman's presence was demanding, her energy intense and focused. This woman was beyond beautiful and clearly intelligent. Confidence dripped from every woven fibre of her stylish suit.

My barrister was everything that I needed. She understood. When she saw me, I knew that for her, it was the final piece in the puzzle. There was only so much you could know about someone, from case notes.

My barrister took me into a consultation room where I was greeted by her assistant and someone else. My barrister explained that this was going to be a short debrief before we were called in. We all sat down. My barrister wasted no time. She stared into my eyes, looking right through me.

As she opened her mouth to speak, I started to lose control. My emotions began to bubble to the surface. As I tried to push my feelings back down, my body began to shake. Tears started rolling down my cheeks uncontrollably. My barrister, still staring right at me, commanded 'stop!' and smiled. She found me, and she found the case.

My barrister's voice changed, and in an almost undetectable urban tone, she said, "girl, you need to wipe those tears." She told me that I had come here to win, and my whole family's future was on the line. Suddenly, she was speaking officially again like the last statement had never happened.

For a minute, I was not just her client. I was a fellow female, fighting to relinquish ownership of the person she had been taught she was. That one line was all I needed. The authentic realness that she gave me was the glue that I needed to hold myself together. I felt a surge in power. She was right.

I had not fought my whole life to get to this point to crumble. I remembered my life as a child. I remembered being a prisoner. I remembered being used, abused, and beaten like I was not worth fundamental human rights. I remembered being locked in bedrooms, wondering if my mum was alive. I remembered my daughter's dad attacking me, drawing blood, calling me damaged, and reminding me that I would never have or be anything.

I put everything into perspective and found my reality. I had researched; I knew what I was talking about, I was working from a place of love and honesty, and I was ready to go.

The case itself was not that bad. There was only one question that the judge asked, that he needed information that had not been submitted in the documents. I had provided my solicitor with this information, and he had not put it in, for reasons unknown to me.

Apart from the one missing piece of information, the months of research and planning I had personally done had really paid off. I could answer all the judge's questions.

My daughter's dad, on the other hand, had researched nothing. Unfortunately, he had come into court with the sole argument that he was her dad, which meant she should stay in this country.

My daughter's dad was asked why he did not believe that she would have a better standard of living in the new country. The judge wanted particulars from him, i.e., would her education be of a lesser standard? Would she have access to more or less of things in the new country?

He could not answer any of the judge's questions at all. When asked how he felt about coming over to see her in the new country, he replied that he felt nothing and would not be coming over if we left.

After a while on the stand, the judge started getting annoyed at my daughter's dad's lack of answers to his questions. This triggered her dad to reveal his genuine attitude. He became aggressive.

As the session ended, I did not feel confident. The judge was a man, a father, and probably a grandfather. I saw him frustrated with my daughters' father for the lack of research he had done, but I also saw him sympathise with his fight to keep his daughter in her country of birth.

I wondered as I waited, how many court cases go the opposite way, to how they are expected to go? The people that decide these judgments are human, and humans can never be entirely objective. I sat in the corridor quietly, trying to control my racing mind. I looked across to where my daughter's father sat, but he refused to catch my eye.

THE CONFIRMATION

I want to backtrack a little. While waiting for the verdict, I reflected on the things that had influenced me in times of uncertainty.

This whole immigration dream had begun with a question. Could I dare to not just ask but demand more for myself and my kids? Could we? Should we? I do not know why I wanted more; you would think that being free would be enough for me. Was I free?

My environment, in general, was not conducive to growth. I was not planted in soil that was nourishing physically or mentally. I wondered what my kids could hope for as they grew up. I realized that no matter how I tried, no matter how well my kids performed in the education system, the chances of them removing themselves from all that they have grown up around would be slim to none.

I had an undeniable hunger for more. The desire was innate. It is the base reason as a child, I questioned being dumped into this existence. All the desire needed was a dream and a focus of energy. This hunger would soon have me feeling like the impossible was possible.

One of the things that contributed to me imagining more was a piece of media that I randomly came across around 2008. It was a cheesy documentary/film about a young lady going through a life of unhappiness and unfulfillment. The docufilm used the woman's life challenges and occurrences to explain the physics of quantum mechanics.

The docufilm was poorly made but perfect in nature. There was no silky-smooth production, but it managed to explain complex concepts in a way that even a layperson like myself could understand.

The docufilm was called '*What the bleep do we know?*' This docufilm based around quantum physics, inspired me to start asking questions again. This time it was not questions surrounding 'why me?' Instead, I started asking questions such as 'what is reality?' 'What is real?' and 'what is not real?'

This arena of introductory quantum physics provided me with the possibility that there was a place between the logic of science and the subjectivity of spirituality. I had been stuck in the logical, heavy world of matter; how could I have been anywhere else?

I had never had opportunities to wonder past the confines of my situation, believe in miracles, or have faith in something higher. All I had known was unanswered prayers. I wanted to believe, but my rational mind had to see it to believe it.

Quantum physics gave me something to believe in without committing to religion, either traditional or new age. Religion of any kind seemed soft to me, and I prided my adult self on being a realist and an atheist. I was surviving real life because of me, not because of a deity that had never shown up before.

I found 'What the bleep do we know,' so refreshing because it placed accountability for what was going right or wrong in our lives back in our hands. I felt for the first time that I was not at the mercy of the outside world.

I had spent my life living reactionary, waiting to see what happened. I expected the worst, and the worst happened.

'*What the bleep do we know,*' introduced the notion that there was scientific evidence to suggest that we create our own realities. The film described how the brain does not distinguish between imagined/remembered things and present reality. It described particles being able to be in two places at once until you observe them. The docufilm explained that all possibilities are available until we settle our attention on one and lock it in as reality. This film opened a whole new realm for me. Could I change my reality? Could I take back control of my life?

At the time of watching this film, I was still in university. I was a single parent, already going against my projected path. The documentary made me ask, should I change what I expected? Although I felt like I was winning, I was still living with my trauma switch on. I always expected something to go wrong or something bad to happen.

When I watched this film, I had never heard of the word manifestation before. It would be an integral part of my life and a global trend in society in the years to come.

After 'What the bleep do we know,' my old view of my reality quickly crumbled, and new concepts were born.

Another docufilm that contributed to my development during that time was '*The Secret.*' The Secret came when I needed it the most. It was around two0twelve and the beginning of our visa Olympics. The Secret told me I could have anything that I wanted in this world. It just had to be what I really wanted. This film highlighted real-life stories of people healing chronic illnesses, people going from having nothing to everything, and miracles taking place.

The Secret is based on the premise that 'thoughts make things and belief. I really wanted this Visa. Deep down in my soul, I believed that what I wanted was part of my life path and would mean a better life for my kids. I had only just started the visa process while watching 'The Secret.' Still, I quickly found myself putting it into practice.

Just like *'What the Bleep Do We Know,'* *'The Secret,'* also championed the notion that we create our realities. In *'What the bleep do we know,'* the focus was on us, limiting our own possibilities of happiness. We do this by reliving negative experiences and thoughts. *'The Secret'* focused on the law of attraction. The law of attraction is a natural law that stipulates that what you send out is what you receive.

It seems a simple notion, but this was mind-blowing to me, who at the time was a champion worrier. This film was crucial because I was currently travelling into the visa Olympics filled with fear.

Another bombshell I received from this film was that the universe does not discriminate between *I do,* and *I do not* want. This meant that every time I had a hurdle to jump for the visa, I went into it with positive statements instead of praying that it did not fail.

Thoughts, I learned, had their own frequencies that were measurable with scientific equipment. Thoughts, like words, leave you as energy and go out into the universe. What you say and think about the most is what creates your reality. You attract what you are sending out.

After watching this film, I vowed to commit to this dream. I knew deep down it was not just a random whim; how could it be? Surely, if that were the case, I would have picked something a little more achievable, it was meant to be.

I had to have confidence in the dream moving forward and have faith that the universe has a plan. What was meant to be would be. I also vowed to remember that this dream would affect people's lives, like my daughter's father. I started to monitor my thoughts, and I brushed the dust off my imagination.

I began to bring my dream to life in my mind. Each time I imagined it, I added another layer, a smell, or a sound, making it seem even closer to reality. I would picture the two youngest kids riding their little tykes' cars down the large hallways and around the big open plan living room. I saw the beach and the kids splashing around. I could smell the BBQ that we would be having for lunch.

I passed the first hurdle of the visa; I was so happy. It was the first significant 'Yes,' a confirmation that I was heading in the right direction. The second hurdle, gaining state sponsorship, was a massive one. This could have gone horribly wrong as it involved my current employer. I had not told my employer that I was trying to leave the country. I had to get the PA of my boss to email the authority, the information they needed; he managed it without causing any drama.

I remember walking to work that day, knowing the visa people had requested further information, knowing I would have to get the PA to intercept the email. Knowing it could all end here. I began to chant in my head, 'everything works out in my best interest.' This mantra became crucial to the entire process. I maintained confidence in the dream. I trusted that if I did not get the outcome that I wanted at any point, despite my best efforts, it would be in my best interest, even if it did not feel like it. With this mantra, I could not fail.

I had successfully passed the skills check and selected the occupation that I qualified for that was in need in the new country, which was a vocational (college) teacher. I gained state sponsorship, and we all passed the medical. All that remained now was to sit back and wait on the list to be granted our visas. We could not just sit back as the court fight was now in full swing.

Life was a rollercoaster. In between wins were painful times; my daughter's father thought I was doing all of this to spite him; he had forgotten who I was. I was not a vindictive person and never once purposely tried to come between him and my daughter. I never argued with him in front of her. I never spoke ill about him around or to her. I kept adult business to the adults. He would not believe that I was still trying to protect his reputation for his daughter.

By the time we got to the final court date, I was broken. Although we were blessed with wins, the seriousness of going to court was too much for me. No number of mantras could soothe me now.

As I waited for the verdict, I remembered making the first phone call to a very reputable visa agent. The agent would have cost thousands of pounds to take care of the visa application. I called them inquiring about my chance of qualifying for a visa. I was told I did not have enough points to apply, and the likelihood of it being granted if I muster enough points were slim to none. I took that information, did my own research, applied for my own Visa, and eventually was granted that Visa. It really could have all ended there and then, during that phone call.

We were all called back into court. My daughter's father and I stood in front of the judge. As he summarised the information that we gave him, he gave nothing away in his face. As he moved into his decision, I felt time slow down, my legs feeling weak. I beg them to bear with me.

The judge talked as if he felt sorry for my daughter's dad. He felt sorry for him because he had not really given him much to work with. The judge then said something to me about missing information and continued looking through papers. I felt like his tone was one of deliberation, and I could not take it.

He looked at me and told me that he had granted me permission to remove my daughter from this jurisdiction. I let out a loud breath that I had clearly been holding and collapsed in tears into the arms of my barrister.

The joy was short-lived. The lack of emotion on his face as he walked out of the court made me shiver.

I had fully considered the implications of going for this dream. I knew the pain it would cause, not just for him but for my husband and me. We were leaving everyone and everything behind which we had ever known. Despite all of this, I did not care. I did not care about anyone other than my kids. Even my own husband was dispensable at this point in comparison to my kids. That did not mean I did not love him; I just loved my children more.

I was fighting for a better future for them. I was fighting to offer the option of a different life. Even if, in the end, they did not want it and returned to our home country. I needed to know that I had placed them in fertile soil, that I had put them somewhere they could grow, thrive, and be safe. I wanted to place them where they would feel, what it was to be young and carefree. That is what I was fighting for, and I won.

YOU COULD NOT WRITE IT

The last court case was in November 2013. All our possessions were loaded into a shipping container and sent off on its three-month journey across the ocean. Our flight tickets had been brought, and we were due to make our getaway on the fourteenth of February two0fourteen. The kids were super excited, and so were we. It was bittersweet because I knew the pain that her father would be feeling.

My daughter's dad and his family made it clear that they were suffering. There was not anything that I could really do about it.

One morning in January, we had a knock on the door; there stood two very official-looking women. My heart dropped, and I fell into a trauma response. Any other person would have just answered the door, but I expected extremes from the life I had lived. *What had my daughter's dad done? What new level of low had he stooped to stop us from going?*

I was scared out of my mind. We had already had child protection involved, and although it was only a precautionary measure, it was not something that I ever wanted to repeat. Thoughts raced through my mind as I paced up and down, trying to figure out what to do. Had the court changed their mind? I did not answer the door, and eventually, they left. As they were going, I heard what sounded like a police radio. I slowly slid down the front door and into a ball, holding my knees close to my chest as tears rolled into my mouth. The car pulled off, and I let out a simpering cry. It was plain-clothed police that had been knocking on the door.

My husband and mum were at work, so I called my sister, who told me to come over. I took myself and the three kids over to hers. When I got there, I told her all about what had happened. I was a mess, pacing, my heart was beating fast, and it would not settle.

I went into her kitchen and poured myself a brandy. It was ten am, but I did not know what else to do to calm my nerves. I tipped the straight brandy back, scrunching my face as it made its way, burning down my throat.

My mobile began to ring. An unknown number, I ignore it, and it continues to ring, only pausing to bypass the 'leave a message' recording. I knew it was not going to stop, so I answered.

The person on the other end said, 'hello, this is Sergeant someone.' The officer explains that she is calling about my daughter's father as he was involved in an incident. A small sigh of relief leaves my body. *What trouble had he got himself into now?*

After a pause that seemed forever, the officer told me that my daughter's father is currently in hospital and in a critical state. I was silent; this was not real. The officer asked me if I was at home. I told her no. The officer asked for my sister's address and said they would send a car to take us to the hospital.

Within only minutes, they had pulled up outside my sister's house. I do not know what I said to my daughter. I was not really thinking straight. It was all happening so fast. I held her hand as tight as I could, and as we got into the back of the police car, I pulled her close to me. The female officer that was not driving started speaking. She is prepping my daughter for what she will see. I am busy staring at my daughter, trying to give her my best 'everything's going to be ok' smile. I only catch the odd word here and there, tubes, machines and asleep. She told my daughter that her dad was put to sleep for his own benefit. I was in disbelief. He was big physically and personality wise; he was loud and intimidating. I could not understand how he could be in such a bad way. My daughter was not panicking at all.

When we got to the hospital, all his friends and family were already there. My daughter's grandma gave her a big hug and sat her down. I was taken into a consultation room by a nurse. She explained that my daughters' father had participated in an argument while outside a bar; the person he was arguing with had punched him in the face and knocked him off balance. Her dad had fallen to the ground and hit his head on the concrete. He was unconscious when the ambulance arrived and was bleeding on the brain. As the pressure in his head built up, he was induced into a comma.

For the next two weeks, my daughter and I sat at his bedside, hoping for it to be the day they could wake him up. Waiting for him to be able to breathe without the life support machine, waiting to hear his big bellowing laugh, as he declares that we cannot get rid of him that easy. The day did not come.

He was deteriorating. Despite all that had transpired between us, I realized that we were family, and we were going to lose him. As bad as things got between us, he was always there. Had there ever been an emergency, he would not think twice about coming to my rescue. His overbearing control when it came to our daughter kept me on my toes, always having to put a case forward for a decision; he had to do the same too. He was like a security net for my parenting, and I was for his.

Looking at him lying in that bed lifeless, apart from the slow rise of his chest, every time the machine commanded, did not seem real. My daughter did not show any emotion at all. She seemed hopeful and spent her days making cards and talking to his friends. She told him often that she loved him.

Unsurprisingly, his mum and dad aged ten years during those two weeks. While sitting at the side of my daughters' dads' bed one day, I heard the scene that another family was having. There was a peaceful silence and then a sudden shrill cry of sorrow as the person slipped away. As I held his hand heavy and swollen, I promised him that if he could wake up for our daughter, I would make things better.

THE LAST GOODBYE

On the fourteenth day, there was a meeting called with his family, which I also sat in on. It was decided that his life-support would be turned off and he would be let go off. I do not know how this was explained to my daughter; it was all a bit of a haze. I know a lovely nurse came and brought her beautiful storybooks about dying. We read them together.

My mum and best friend were able to come and support us. We were all there for each other and, more importantly, for my daughter and his parents.

Time was different now. It was running out, and we started saying our goodbyes. The adults tried to hold it together for my daughter, but she seemed to be managing it better than all of us. I promised him that I would make sure that his daughter had the absolute best life she could. I promised him that I would always keep his name alive in our household.

When the time came close, my daughter cried. I am not sure if she cried because of the death or the sadness of watching it all unfold. How much grief can a ten-year-old really process?

It is the same with most childhood traumas. At the time of the trauma, you are only aware of the surface. We must wait until we have emotional understanding and the vocabulary to process it. As a child, you do not even have the words to explain your feelings.

The time came for the life machine to be turned off. We all sat around, touching him, and holding his swollen hands. My daughter was stroking his face calmly, and then came the noise. The flatline. I selfishly and unexpectedly burst into a panic attack. I cried so hard and so fast that I could not catch a breath.

I am not sure why I reacted like that. It was because our relationship had used and created so much energy. The relationship was a massive part of who I had been and who I would become. It had been all I had known since I was sixteen years old. To witness my daughter's dad's last breath, leave his body was a shock. I had expected him to be in me and my daughters' lives forever, negative, or not. I remember looking at his chest deflate for the last time, then at my daughter's face, and that was that.

I suddenly felt a heavy sense of responsibility, like I was incapable of raising this child by myself. My forgotten lack of confidence in myself as a parent reared its anxious head. I had relied on his control without realizing it. Now that control was gone.

Unfortunately, my family and I had to choose whether we should stay for the funeral or leave when the flights were already booked for. I asked my daughter what she wanted to do. I told her that she and I could go to the funeral and then follow my husband and the younger two kids after. My daughter decided that she did not need to be at the funeral to say goodbye to her dad. She had already done that at his bedside. Her reasoning made complete sense to me.

The only reason I could see to stay and go to the funeral was for the 'look' of it, for my daughter to be there for everyone to see. I was not about to make her do something she did not want to do for other people's benefits or because that is 'traditionally' done. There was no need for her to see her dads' body be put in the ground and watch all his friends and family breakdown. I saw no benefit in my daughter watching all the adults she looked up to for strength, including myself, breaking around her.

His family became over involved in our departure, asking me questions I did not have answers for. The pressure that my daughter's family tried to impart me brought me to the point of feeling like I was running away again.

I felt stressed, but not enough to change my mind. I could not take this trauma away for my daughter, but I could get her the hell out of here and into her new life.

CHAPTER FIVE

$\iff$

A Not So Fresh Start

SADNESS AND JOY

We arrived in our new country of residence fresh from the death of my daughters' father and still in shock. The plane journey was the accumulation of eighteen months' worth of fight, a lost life, and all that I believed. When we walked out of the airport, the dense, comforting heat hit our faces. I felt a group sigh of relief. For months, the adventure of exploring this new land was enough to keep us occupied. We visited terrains we had never seen before. We saw animals we had only seen on the TV. We went to beautiful local beaches every day and marvelled at the clear display of stars every night. My daughter had always been strong and logical minded. She lived in her own world with her own rules.

I feared at first that my daughter had flipped the switch on her emotions to self-preserve. We decided to do a course of counselling. It was beneficial up to a point, and she seemed okay. When her counsellor could no longer see her, my daughter made it clear that she did not need to start seeing someone else, so the counselling stopped.

Over the next few years, I did not think so much about the switch that I believed my daughter had turned off. With two younger kids to look after and the enormous goal of creating the absolute best childhood I could for them all, I was kept busy. In the beginning, a sense of achievement that we had made it and my love of being a mum kept me fulfilled.

Far before the death of my daughters' father, I had vowed that I would do anything and everything I could to make sure that my eldest daughter succeeded in this life. This bold statement was the start of the pressure I would not only put on myself but on her. This statement arose out of my own personal guilt. I felt like I had not changed the cycle. When I gave birth to her, all I wanted was a 'normal' family set up, the kind I had dreamt of as a child. This dream was why I clung to her dad so tightly in the early days. I had not seen a family like his before. I had failed to give her this, and it slowly smouldered a hole in my heart. Not only could I not provide her with a traditional family set up but now she had to go through the complete loss of a parent.

My daughter and I plodded along for the next few years, really having what others would call a 'normal' relationship. She played with her friends, went to school, and sometimes misbehaved like any other child.

It was not until puberty hit, that things for us changed. At this point, I wish someone had told me that it was not my job to diagnose and decide how my daughter's life would be. I believed that if you got the foundations right well before a child becomes a teen, it would be a pain-free process. I saw myself as a cool, laid-back kind of mum with great boundaries and reasonable expectations.

I thought that if I just kept talking to her, it would all be okay. She trusted me, so I should be able to advise her and have her listen. I had done an excellent job of keeping her alive this far. I did not see why I could not walk her through her teenage years while helping her reach her full potential.

I decided that my daughter would excel in high school, breeze through college, graduate university, bestowing on me the final 'look at what a good mum I am' medal of honour. Looking back now, I was very naïve. The chances of the plan being executed without any issues were minuscule.

My problem was that I was coming from a very extreme childhood. In my mind, if I made sure my kids' childhood was as far away from that as possible, they would have happy and successful lives. What I did not consider looking back was that childhood was hard to navigate, even without trauma.

The speed at which society was evolving into something that was not only superficial but judgmental was extremely scary. Our children are up against body shaming, highly sexualised clothes/TV/music, and celebrities on pedestals void of any actual talent. They are fighting with snap chat, Tik Tok, Instagram, drugs, peer pressure, parent pressure, school pressure, raging hormones, fearmongering, and divorce.

I was up against more than I realised. To make matters worse, my trauma encouraged me to take the parenting of a teen journey personally.

IT TAKES A VILLAGE

My daughter is seventeen now, and I am still not sure if her behaviour over her teen years was due to trauma, puberty, isolation, or a combination of them all. The isolation was the primary factor in creating the pressure cooker environment that we ended up with. We had no close family in the new country, which meant that my daughter had no one to run to when she had had enough of me.

My goals and dreams of a better life abroad honestly did not consider the need for trusted people in our lives. It did not cross our minds because we had never needed anyone before. This was true even while in our home country; I realise now that we did not need people before because we had not had a teenager yet.

By the time my daughter was a teenager, she had shown little emotion regarding her dad's death. I still talked to her about her dad, and she was okay with that. She just never got upset.

Because of this lack of perceived grief, by the time she started acting up, I was ready to put it down to good old bad behaviour.

The belief that she was fine and was just a challenging child started to slip away the further into puberty she went. I failed to account for puberty. My daughter and I rode the puberty waves without causing too much damage. We endured the hormone fuelled fights that were constantly blown out of proportion. In these blow-ups, we both expressed our past and current pain.

I had no point of reference. People say, "you know what it's like to be a teen," or "that's just a teen thing," you were one once, but I did not. I had not known what it was like to be a teen. I had never had the freedom to vocalise my despair, feel low energy and hide in my personal space listening to depressing music. I had never fantasised about crushes or been heartbroken because the crush did not return my affections. I had never been able to be angry at the world because I had to wash dishes. I did not know what it was like because I did not have a childhood.

I thought that I managed life quite well, considering the trauma I had endured as a child and a young adult. In my younger days, the only evidence of the life I had lived would be in the odd drink-fuelled arguments with someone on a dance floor, or if a bouncer was being a bully, then you would see anger.

The last decade had been hectic for me. I had been busy fighting battles. I never really had the time to really look at myself. After the first year in our new country, the novelty began to wear off, I noticed a problem. The problem was my periods. For two weeks out of the month, I felt like a completely different human being. I was short-tempered, easily agitated, and I was low patience. Only having two standard weeks out of the month became almost unbearable.

My daughter had her own raging hormones. The more I got wrong with her, the more I let the excuse of hormones rule my reactions, the more I would beat myself up for not doing and being a better parent. The wheels of my trauma cycle had begun to turn. This time I was my own enemy. After a visit to my GP to have blood tests, I found out my hormones were completely normal. I could no longer use hormones alone as the excuse for my pain and behaviour there was clearly more to it.

ROCK BOTTOM

It was New Year's Eve 2019, and we had been at my friend's New Year's Eve party. I had been drinking a little, and we had had a lovely time. We had come back from the party, and my eldest daughter had done or said something. Before I knew it, we were arguing. Voices elevated; shots of angry frustrations exchanged.

She wanted me to be different, and I wanted her to change. We both believed the other person's change would make our lives happy, and then we would be better. Each of us could not understand why the other person would not just make the change for the love of the other. Neither of us realised that it was impossible to make someone change. If a person were supposed to change, they could only learn why they should change, the natural way through trials and tribulations. Without personal motivation, no change can be made.

For the first time, the younger two kids became fearful and sought safety in the arms of my husband, who was trying to calm the situation down. When I looked at my two younger kids' faces and saw the fear, instead of displaying the upset and shame I felt, out came the rage.

I snapped and told my daughter to get out. It was ten past twelve midnight, and she rightfully refused to leave. Eventually, after the arguing continued, I physically dragged her out of the front door and threw her out.

Less than five minutes later, the red mist that had seemed to saturate me began to clear, and I regained a sense of the present. What was I doing? What was I thinking? I ran straight outside and called her name; she did not answer, and I did not know where she was. We frantically looked everywhere; her stepdad went out in the car to check the surrounding streets.

I finally found her hidden down the side of the house. I pleaded with her to come in. She looked angry, but eventually, she came in, and I went to bed. That night I cried and cried and cried some more. I did not know what to do.

I knew that as much as teens were complex and sometimes hurtful, I was not the victim. I had needed her to meet me halfway in her behaviour. All avenues had been exhausted. I had employed meaningful consequences instead of punishments, and I had tried my best to keep communication open and honest. I had tried setting boundaries, taking her phone, giving her spends, taking her spends, and none of it seemed to work. My daughter's behaviour was not changing, only becoming worse, and I could not control my reactions to that behaviour.

I cried every tear I could squeeze out of my wrung heart that night. I had hit rock bottom. I had enough of falling and having to get back up. My lack of control would result in days of mental self-beatings. I had failed again. She was a teenager, a child still. She would always overreact, which is why she needed me to be something I could not.

She needed the gentle mother my mum had been for me, while I thrashed around in my hormones and pain. Throughout the whole build-up to her being a teenager, I never thought I had a problem. I knew I struggled with my moods during my periods, but I thought my pain came from having the stress of a teenager who wanted to argue with me all the time.

Before New Year. I had been trying to get a grip of my period, and I was making satisfactory progress. I was doing things that were good for my growth, like reading about the mind, trauma, and overcoming pain. I learned about meditating and started keeping fit.

It appeared that every time I started to make progress with gaining control of my emotions, my daughter would unintentionally trigger me back to the beginning. Before I knew it, I would be back in the cycle. I would react, overreact, and then go and quietly beat myself up.

That New Year event was rock bottom for me because I had dragged my daughter out of my front door. I was ashamed, and I was broken. At that point, something clicked in me. I realised that I needed to focus on taking a long honest look at myself. Do not get me wrong, I had tried to be better the whole time, but it was only surface better. I needed to find the underlying cause of my own behaviour. If I could not change how I reacted when triggered, then I knew I would not survive, and worse, I would not have a relationship left with my daughter.

I had spent the last two years trying to modify my daughter's behaviour while slightly working on mine. I had tried, begged her to make choices that helped me be triggered less often. This was wrong. I was wrong to expect a teenager to help me, an adult, when I could not even help myself.

I learned that day on New Year that when a relationship is in turmoil, you cannot focus on the other person. The light at the end of the pain is that each one of us has the definite potential to change ourselves. We cannot change someone else because that challenge and the subsequent prize is their birth right and journey. From that New Year, the self-work I had been doing on and off became a full-time commitment spanning the next three years. The pledge was not to be a better parent but a whole better me.

I made a pact to meet myself, the good, the bad, and the ugly. The first thing I did was step up my reading; luckily, it was something I already enjoyed. There was something magical about reading books that authors sometimes spent lifetimes putting together, books that were born out of a unique human being's life experience.

Over the next few months, I learned that my mind was not my friend. This revelation was personality destroying. When it was not clouded with emotional fog, my mind was the one thing of which I was proud. I prided myself on my ability to think and understand. I had excelled in school and graduated university twice as a single parent.

I did not realise how much more headspace I could have access to without the junk. This junk included: constant life narrations, imagined psychic abilities that allowed me to know negative things that people were thinking about me, and the continuous foretelling of adverse events.

By the summer after the New Year's Eve event, I was practising daily meditation. Every morning before everyone else rose, I would sit outside and meditate in peace. One morning after meditating, I found myself crying softly. I looked at myself in my phone camera, the corners of my mouth began to reach up and out, and I began to smile. My cheeks began to shake and tremble. I cried some more. I had been so consumed with the stress and pressure of life that I had clearly forgotten how to be present. I had either stopped smiling or never began. If an authentic, big smile could cause my facial muscles to freak out, then I had been in a bad way.

During the next seven months, I made considerable progress in making my new choices become habits. I maintained a conscious observation of my thoughts and slowly began to experience bouts of peace of mind. The effects of my periods were now minimal; although still present, I was calmer. Me and my daughter's relationship improved, we still had arguments, but they happened less often. Just as my eldest daughter and I felt we had crossed a bridge together, we started to have issues with school.

A SQUARE PEG IN A ROUND HOLE

The New Year was peaceful in the house. It was also full of excitement as my mother came over from our home country. I had decided that while she was here, I would try and create a type of lifetime line and ask her for help with any missing dates. My mother came during January, and we had a wonderful time. It was like we had not been apart. The kids quickly melted back into her warm rays.

I could not ask her any deep questions regarding my childhood, just asking her what dates we lived in certain homes was enough to send her into tears. I did not want to upset her. She had looked me in the eyes and broke down in tears, proclaiming that she would never be able to forgive herself. I stared back at her, into her soul, smiled, and told her that she had to.

In my study of people and trauma, I had learned that the trauma we endured was not personal to us; it was his story playing out, his cycle. Our recovery was our story. We cannot describe our lives as a horror story and then beat ourselves up for being there. The visit from my mother was profoundly rejuvenating for us all.

February was the start of a new school year for my eldest. After a much better summer holiday, I had hoped for an improved effort from her. These hopes were quickly shattered. Only weeks into the new school year, and I was already receiving emails and phone calls, I would not mind, but it was regarding trivial issues. Trivial or not, every time I responded to an email or took another call, my frustration would start to bubble. Talking in class, missing deadlines, answering back, and those were the days she made it into school.

The arguments about school built up over the next nine months to daily. I could not understand why she would do this to us. We only had one wage coming in and prioritised her education over holidays and trips. That was our decision. However, to see her not even trying to make it work was upsetting, to say the least. My anger would shout at her, calling her ungrateful. I would make her feel bad because of the sacrifices we chose to make. I am ashamed to say that I went as far as to tell her that her deceased father would be rolling in his grave if he could see her now. We may have been quite different people, but me and her dad both agreed on how important her education was. The arguments on occasion would turn into fights because I would take the only thing she cared about away from her, her phone. She and I would wrestle as I tried to ply the phone from her hands. My daughter started to hate school more and attend less. I knew deep down that this school situation was another learning area for me. I had done self-work, but clearly thought I was further along than I was.

Although the school situation was not new, it was intensifying. No matter how hard things got, no matter how I neglected the tools, I had learned, one thing I did not stop doing was reflecting. I asked myself questions, and I tried to answer them.

I now believed that the only block to complete peace was this school situation. In effect, I was still living reactionary to situations. No matter how far I thought I had come, I was only doing well while not triggered. My success was still dependent on things going smoothly.

Incidents happened that year at school that were not my daughters' fault, or she would be picked out and made an example of for an incident involving tens of students. These times I would go to war with the school. I would pull their own policies out and write ten-page complaints regarding their handling of the situation. Despite my frustrations, I had her back, but I was also being worn down.

School was a constant issue in our lives; it was always something, whether her fault or not. The more that school complained, the bigger the feeling of failing her became. The more I felt like I was letting her down, the more pressure I put on her to comply.

I needed a win, her win. My daughter's success at school would be a marker that I had won the fight against the effects of her trauma, so I could rest. This need of mine, along with all that society asked for and expected, was breaking her. I was no longer thinking clearly. I cried each night, and sleep dwindled too hardly anything. The less energy I had, the more my patience was reduced. I was no longer doing the things that were good for my mental health.

THE UNWORTHY FIGHT

I want to bring you to today, two0twoone. We sometimes have people that are acquaintances. Over the years, you get into the habit of stopping to say hi and enjoy a quick surface chat. You sense they have good energy, but it never goes any further. I had a friend like that. She was a mum at our primary school and had a son in my younger daughters' class. The mum also had an older son in the same high school my eldest daughter had attended.

The last few years of high school that I described previously had been so stressful that I would burst into tears when asked how she was doing. All the mums I spoke to knew of our battles. This mum always asked me how she was and until this year two0twoone, I had little positive to update.

This time though, when she asked me how she was, I replied, "fantastic." I told her that my daughter had found herself a traineeship at a Montessori childcare centre. She was sixteen, soon to be seventeen in a month, and was earning good money while studying on the job.

My daughter had always had a way with younger kids and was a sought-after babysitter. The mum I was talking to looked shocked and interested. She was shocked because the aim of the game, if you were any type of good parent, was to keep your kid in school right until the very end, eighteen years old, no matter what. If your kid could not make it to the end, then you and your kids were looked upon with sadness. Going to a technical college and learning a trade instead of staying at school and doing another two years of general education (only to leave at the end with little) was also seen as failing, which was ridiculous.

I told my friend that my and my daughter's relationship was now fantastic, but I could have easily lost it. All because of the pressure of school. I tell the mum that I had spent the last two years fighting with my daughter over school. Stuck in a cycle of fighting with her and then fighting myself for my lack of self-patience. I told her how many nights, I had spent crying in my bedroom, beating myself up. The mum suddenly began to sob understandingly. I gave her a big hug and, while smiling, told her that she was not the only one.

The friend went on to describe the same situation we had been in. Both her and her partner, worked numerous jobs, to send their son to that school; they thought his behaviour showed ungratefulness. They could not understand why he could not do what they asked of him. She explained how there was no relationship left with him. It had gotten that bad that they considered letting him leave school at year ten to do something else. I told her that leaving the institution of school, was not necessarily a terrible thing for some kids.

I told her that I wished someone had told me that high schools do not really care before giving so much of my family's energy to it. It is not malicious; it is business. Schools are there to teach what the government wants your kids to know and teach it in the most cost-effective way, ticking as many boxes as they can per task. Schools teach to the majority. Like anything in society, the majority rules.

Most kids are compliant; most kids are round pegs that fit perfectly into the round holes of school. The only problem is that every so often along comes a kid that is a square peg. In my case, I had created my square peg without even realising it.

I had taught her to be an individual, to use her own brain, and question everything. I had taught her how to communicate her thoughts with precision. In my own actions, I had shown her that the traditional way was not the only path.

My daughter was sick of the teacher's nit-picking. She was sick of teachers who were not bothered about the students but still expected them to pander to their god complexes. She was sick of being told to do things just for the sake of doing them. She was sick of being treated like she did not deserve to have an opinion and was not old enough to question.

I was clearly not aware at the time; of the part I had played in creating who she was; all I could hear and see was that we were failing. The truth was we were failing the impossible mission. We were forcing a square peg into a round hole. I told my mum friend that schools do not care about the impact of the seven emails a day they feel they must send. They do not care about parents' mental health, the relationship between the parent and child, or the overall effect on the family; they must tick admin boxes. I shudder to think if the school system were this quick to contact home in my childhood days, I would have not survived.

The scary thing is that millions of children are still living with an abusive parent just waiting for an excuse, but hey, at least the school has done its job. I told my friend to follow her gut and let her son leave school. Her younger son was highly academic and would one day flourish in the current education system; that is the point.

All our kids are not the same, but the school system tries to convince us that they are, and if they are not, there is something wrong with them, and us as parents. I told my friend not to give the school system any more of her tears or her relationship with her son. The point of life is to find peace and happiness. This is not found in a qualification or a job; it is not found in anything external.

THE LAST STRETCH ON A RUBBER BAND

For the last term of the year, my daughter started a new school. She felt like her time at her current school had run its course. At first, when she said she not only wanted to move to a new school, but she wanted to try a public school, I was not happy. My ego said things to me like, "after all the tears you have both cried, you are just going to bail out? After all the money we have invested, she is not even going to finish year ten?"

When we started listening to her, we realised that she put forward a good argument. She said that if we let her go to a public school, we would have less money to pay out. She explained that with less money to pay out for schooling, there would be a little less pressure put on her to succeed, and this change would result in her success.

She also stated that it was not the school that made the child achieve, but the child itself, and if she were going to do well, she would do well in any school. How could I argue with that? It was the truth.

My daughter told us about a public school, with an ok reputation and stated that she knew someone there. It was out of the boundary, but we managed to get her in. She started school during the last term of the year so that she could settle in before the summer holidays and the new school year.

Within a week of starting that new school, she was bullied for the first time ever. She was bullied horrendously for two weeks straight; she was physically threatened, intimidated, and humiliated. These two weeks were followed by three weeks' worth of going backwards and forwards between her and her teachers.

My daughter was traumatised by the events and gave up. I tried to get her to go back to school, and sometimes she did for a day or so, but it did not last. I was furious and upset. I had made what seemed like an enormous mistake in letting her leave the old school. I beat myself up; it was easy to do because of my apparent lack of long-term memory.

I had clearly forgotten how hard it had been for her and me at the old school, how she had hated being there despite having a good group of friends. I forgot the wasted money the school had cost and the pressure I had put on her to achieve because of the sacrifices we had made. I forgot all of that and instead decided that I had messed up yet again. I was a terrible mum.

We had a terrible argument that resulted in the usual angry and hurtful things being said on both sides. This argument was different. My daughter had said, "I don't want to be here." It was nothing new in terms of words; however, the feeling behind it was new. She sounded like she meant it. She seemed tired of having the same arguments and fighting the same battles. After the disagreement, I wearily retreated to my room, instead of the ordinary mental beating that I would typically give myself, declaring that she is just a teen and does not understand, I did something new. Instead of silently screaming the question, "how can you shout at her when she's hurting?" and "what the hell is wrong with you?" I lay feeling numb, staring up at my ceiling.

Instead of debating how much of a horrible human being I was, I decided I did not want to be me anymore. I decided this because the 'me' of the present could not be the softly spoken, patient, thick-skinned, but gentle mum that my daughter needed.

In real life (outside of my head), I did everything I could do for her. I was very reactionary, but I had not stopped trying to work on that; my problem was that I was reacting from my own deep-seated pain that was nothing to do with her.

ANTI-DEPRESSANTS FOR A DAY

I knew neither of us could change right now, that I would have to do something drastic to change myself for her. I had tried with all my heart to stop being triggered, and nothing had worked. I needed something to change, and fast, we were coming to a breaking point in our relationship. Soon all that would be left would be the scar. That night, I decided after all my years of self-healing, surviving, and even sometimes thriving, I was going to go to the doctors to ask for some medication.

This was as big a decision for me as it is for everyone that goes down that road. Defeat was not a road I travelled well. I had worked so hard to self-heal holistically. After everything I had endured, the thing that brought me to medication, was arguing with my teenage daughter.

I felt like a failure, not because I wanted to get medication but because I thought that I could work through anything. Working through things, had helped me right up until the point of having a teenage daughter. Now, no amount of reading, meditating, or reflection could help me. This time I needed help.

The day I went to the doctor was very traumatic. Anyone that says people who get medication for mental health, are taking the easy way out, could not be more wrong. Even the short car journey was challenging work. I left everything I needed at home. I sat in the waiting room anxiously waiting until the Dr called me in.

I had to admit that I needed help. I explained my past and my daughters' story, and of course, the doctor agreed to prescribe me a low dose of anti-depression tablets. She also recommended both myself and my daughter start another course of counselling. Sitting in front of a stranger in a cold white room, while revealing my innermost vulnerabilities was painful.

The worst part of that day was going to my local chemist; the head pharmacist, a lovely lady, would always chat with me. This trip to the chemist was different, we exchanged the usual pleasantries, and then I gave her the prescription.

This time the eyes of the chemist met mine with softness and questions. The pharmacist asked me quietly if I had taken this medication before. I said "no" and nonchalantly added, 'I normally prefer the holistic way.' She looked at me and said, 'keep meditating, it comes part and parcel, and it will be good for you,' I had never told her that I meditated.

At that point, I burst into tears, grabbed my prescription, and proceeded to exit the chemist. I went home, and I took the first tablet. I expected drastic chemical change to happen straight away, and luckily it did not.

The following day started as expected, with my morning caramel latte taking centre stage. It was a Saturday, and there was nowhere to rush to; returning to the comfort of my bed was the obvious next move. As the coffee mug made its way up to my lips, lifted by my appreciate hands, the familiar smell hits my nose. *"Hmmmmm, small pleasures."* As the first sip settled on my tongue, I realised it did not taste the same. In fact, it did not taste at all; the bland froth was insulting.

That event produced a flash-forward of my life on anti-depressants. The flash-forward was highly dramatized but felt like a genuine possibility. Not being able to taste my favourite coffee felt like my future on medication. This was a scary thought because although life had been burdensome, it had also been beautiful. The lows had enabled me to find highs in the simplest of things. At times, the polar extremes of vibration would have me feeling like I was riding a rollercoaster, but I still did not want to get off. Did I sometimes feel like I was completely done with the ride? Yes, I did, but when the time came to choose, I was not willing to give up the good for a neutral journey.

The lows had powerful potential and could easily set ripples travelling through my life. The highs could be triggered by usually unnoticed magic. I was able to find beauty in the things we take for granted. When you experience tough times, you begin to appreciate and seek out every bit of happiness, peace, and pleasure you can find. You become more aware of the abundance of these things around you.

I could marvel at a leaf's journey from its branch to where it rests its body on the ground, I could stare at the sky and the clouds for hours in awe, I could smell the grass wafting through the house after the sprinklers had been on while appreciating my very existence on this earth. I could sit on the beach at five am and cry at the innocent calm of the ocean at sunrise. I often watched my kids play like I was watching a movie in blissful slow motion. I was grateful for everything in my life, and that gratitude had come from hardship and pain.

In the experience of not being able to taste my coffee, I decided to still feel, despite the pain. My friend told me about a psychologist that worked at a women's centre that dealt with women that had been through trauma, violence, and abuse. I decided to give that a go first instead of the medication.

Later that day, after my big medication epiphany, I found out that my taste buds had not changed because of taking one anti-depressant; the milk had been off. I sound like a drama queen now, but the experience was authentic to me. The reality of the incident may have been mistaken; however, the insight it gifted me with was clear as daylight. I still have the pack of anti-depressants; it sits in my drawer like a safety blanket. Having the tablets in my draw makes me feel empowered. I know that while I am not taking them, it is because I chose not to. I am making a choice; does that mean I am never going to take them? No, it does not. It just means that I am deciding based on what is right for me here and now.

My daughter did three weeks during the last term of the school year; the bullying died down, but the rumours remained. Before we knew it, we were at the end of the term, and the year was over.

I started to see a counsellor that I really resonated with, and my daughter and I were getting on well. My daughter convinced me that she was feeling okay and that it would be a promising idea to wait to go back to school until after the holidays. After that time, the bullies would have left, and the other people involved would have forgotten all about it. After hearing a convincing case that made sense, we decided to go with her plan.

My mind became at ease with the situation, and we had a very peaceful December and Christmas. My daughter and I spent time together over the summer, which had been mostly positive. Christmas was lovely and unusually drama free. I did not cry or grieve the family that I did not have. I just enjoyed the people I did.

Everything was going well until New Year's Day. Everyone had finished breakfast and had gone to do their own things. My kids were playing with their new toys in the playroom; I went and joined them with my cup of coffee. Sitting on the playroom couch, I watched them, feeling blessed. While smiling at the scene, I found my eyes being drawn to little white bits on the floor. I asked, "Does anyone know what these white bits on the floor are?" Everyone in the house that could hear me replied with no.

I felt a sudden tidal wave of rage rolling up and down my body head to toe. I had never felt such unexpected and intense anger. I tried to shake it off, I had a logical and honest word with myself, but nothing would extinguish the fire. As I sat there, tears now rolling down my cheeks, I realised there was a problem. I was triggered, and it had nothing to do with my eldest daughter.

I took myself back to my bedroom, got into bed, and cried. On hearing the commotion, my husband came in and lay down next to me. He put his arms around me and asked me what was wrong. I replied, feeling pathetic, 'the white bits on the floor.'

CHAPTER SIX

❦

Team Spirit

WELCOME TO MY TRAUMA TEAM

Painful energy had been building up within me. The moment was mine to own, not my eldest daughters, not my younger kids, not my husbands; this was all mine. As I cried in my husband's arms after becoming enraged by the sight of the bits on the floor, I tried to reflect. The rage had simmered down, revealing a glimpse of something else. There was a feeling beneath the rage, and it was not anger. It felt like frustration, intense frustration.

I began to think about my behaviour in the months prior to this event. That which was observed in me did not resonate. Here was someone who was excessive about having a tidy home. Someone who was continuously moaning at and demanding from everyone in the house. I saw someone who obsessively had to fill any family free time by keeping them busy doing some activity or another. All that I was doing, providing, and receiving was never good enough for me.

Who was I trying to keep up with? Was the house not good enough? Was the number of activities I did with the kids not good enough? Am I not good enough as a mum? I wondered where these feelings of inadequacy had come from, I did not feel like my personality really cared about what other people thought. At this stage, my friendship circle had dwindled to almost no one, so there was not even a comparison among my peers. It really did not make sense that this frustration was based on whether I was successful in this society.

We had so much gratitude for all the things in our lives, enough to prevent us from feeling like we lacked anything. We did not have major surpluses in finances, flash cars, and expensive holidays, but we were blessed. The only conclusion to come to was that these feelings were not of this time. I had to go back to the only place where they might have come from, which was my childhood.

There it was, hiding so well you could hardly make it out. My general childhood trauma was the culprit of this mess in which I was buried. The New Year's Eve event lasted two hours from start to finish. By the end of the two hours, I had come to a major epiphany that would springboard my healing journey into rapid drive.

I figured out that I had been operating from expectations that were not mine. Personally, I valued experience, and being present, I saw myself as a relaxed spirit. I was an empath who was able to connect with people on a deeper level. If that were who I was and who I had been becoming for the last few years, why would I lose control over bits on the floor? The answer is simple, it was not me reacting. It was my dad.

Everything made complete sense now. The reason I reacted so badly to my eldest daughters' behaviour, was that I was still holding the expectations that were put on me as a child, in a subconscious filing cabinet somewhere deep in my psyche. The things that triggered me were the general expectations that were put on me as a child not being met.

The reason I would beat myself up after reacting badly to these expectations not being met, was because those expectations did not align with who I was. The expectations were not mine. I was nowhere near as physically abusive as my dad; however, I did regrettably slap my eldest daughter in the face. I do not think this is okay, even in the split seconds of lost tempers, I did not even try and justify it to myself. How could I? What is scary is the fact that so many children like me have the potential to be their parents.

You may think you are nothing like them. You may spend entire lifetimes purposely being the opposite of them, but still a day can come, with the correct conditions and trigger, and there they are within you. If my dad was able to creep on up into my life, with all the self-reflection and learning I had been doing, then there must be millions of adult child abuse survivors going through the same but worse. All those childhood trauma survivors think that they are struggling with themselves when really, they are in a battle with their parents. How had I let this slip by me? Easy, I had been so focused on healing what I deemed 'the big traumas' that I had neglected to assess the impact of my general day to day upbringing, which was actually having a massive effect on how I was living and raising my kids.

At that point, at that moment, I could see now how my trauma team was nearing the end of its completion. It would either submit under pressure, or it would break, and they would turn against me. I remember saying things like, "can you please keep the house tidy; it is bad for my mental health to live in what looks like chaos" I would uncomfortably laugh after this statement knowing full well that it was the truth.

The constant frustration of not being able to run the house or the kids' life's how I wanted to, had built up over the last few weeks prior to New Year's Eve. I had been emotionally blackmailing all the members of my family, including my two younger kids. After telling my younger kids off for doing something wrong, while they were apologising, I would tell them not to say sorry to me because "if you really cared, you would do what I taught you to do" This kind of talk to my kids this would end in a mental beating and guilt for being hard on them.

I would crumble in a pile of tears locked in my room because of my eldest daughter's lack of respect and empathy for how I felt. I just wanted everyone to cooperate so we could all live harmoniously, and my mind could be at peace. I needed more control as my mental health slowly started to decline.

I could see now how it would have become an extremely dangerous spiral for my family and me, had I not realised what was happening. I could see myself being even more dramatic as the weeks and months passed by, getting more upset when someone did not do what I asked them to do and, even worse, how I wanted them to do it. I could imagine my husband being upset and angry because he just could not give me what I wanted. I could see the kids being sad and feeling like failures for not being able to make me happy. None of this was their responsibility. It was mine.

TWO JOURNEYS, ONE TICKET

While I embarked on another round of reflection, my sixteen-year-old daughter had reached a crossroad of her own. This crossroad prompted her to make decisions, one of which was that she would journey back to our country of residence. The expectation of returning to our home country was self-discovery and reconnection to her family, present and past.

The day she was due to leave, she was scared, but she did not show it. I was so proud of her, not because she did not show her fear but because she faced it head-on. She was afraid of being away from me and fearful of what she would find when she got there. Understandably there was an apprehension surrounding attending her dad's grave and seeing her dad's family for the first time in five years. My daughter did not let these worries stop her.

Although I had done my best and spent the last few years really trying to heal myself so that I could be a better parent, I was still being triggered. The situation at home could only be described as living in our own little pressure cooker. The lack of school attendance was causing the temperature to rise consistently. I unintentionally downplayed the bullying which my daughter had received because it was only for two weeks. I now understand that although the bullying seemed mild to me (Wrongly based on my pain endurance levels), it had triggered her emotions and feelings back. The two weeks of bullying she received had re-traumatised her; the threats of being bashed after school left her, considering her dad's fatal death.

Feelings that she had locked far away after her dad's death were suddenly uncontainable. As a result of this, she fell into a mild depression. My daughter had shouted numerous times in arguments, that she wanted to go and be with her family, and every time, I had cried back 'no.' I did not say 'no' out of spite, but I felt it would be better if she waited until she was eighteen. I also wanted her to wait until after she had had another round of counselling here first.

This 'no' eventually turned into a 'not yet 'and then a 'maybe' as I became more worn down with the frustration of not making everything better for her. Every time she shouted that she wanted to leave, I attributed it to her wanting to flee from the situation, which I had let her do before. It occurred to me that this was a lesson that I was supposed to teach about not running away from your problems.

Considering parental responsibilities and that which I was supposed to be 'teaching' had become more of a priority than understanding. I struggled to meet my daughter where she was. The acknowledgement that she had mild depression caused anger within me. After everything that we had overcome, the struggle to move to this beautiful country, the fights to get places at the good schools, the sacrifices. After all the work I had done purely to be a better parent, I still could not save her. I was selfish.

I was correlating her state of mind with how good of a parent I was. I was not treating her like a sovereign human being, a human being with her own path to take, her own pains to overcome, and her own happiness to hold.

As she started her descent into inner turmoil, I could not consistently respond as a trauma-free parent would. I tried my best to communicate to my daughter how much I loved her. Sometimes my fear, anxiety, panic, and frustration got in the way of the light I tried to be for her.

Options for schooling were dwindling, and my daughter was slipping behind. The depression was starting to look like it could become a part of her. Immeasurable pain was born watching my grown child drowning, refusing to raise even a finger of the water for me to hold onto.

A need weighed down heavily on me for my daughter to snap out of the depression; I wanted her to fight for life. I was in the space of wanting to shake and hug her simultaneously. Proclaiming that she was better and stronger than this, did nothing to help her. This job was my most important, and yet no matter how hard I tried, I was unsuccessful at it. I continued making the situation worse.

I had worked on myself so much during the last three years that almost nothing could rile me or trigger me, and here I was reacting like a baby. I read everything I could on psychology, spirituality, pain, suffering and the ego. I meditated, gave up unhealthy habits and ate healthier. I tried to stay as positive as possible, and I managed to turn most situations around with perspective. The only thing that triggered uncontrollable emotions was the happiness of my eldest daughter.

At the beginning of my daughter's life, the pressure bestowed on me was primarily due to my inability to provide her with a traditional family unit. I could not even give her both parents. A vow was taken to make sure that she lived a happy and successful life by any means necessary.

This vow was a heavy pressure to carry. When you have your own children after trauma, you aim to ensure that they do not have to live a life like you had. To an extent, there was success in creating a different life for my daughter; however, just because you removed the trauma that you had, did not necessarily mean that your children would have an unchallenging ride growing up.

There were no comparisons between my childhood and the life I fought for my daughter to have. It was hard for my teen to see things from my point of view, which is how I had subconsciously wanted it. I did not know that my daughter's inability to understand me was due to success in breaking some of our cycles.

I cried about my daughter's lack of empathy; how could she not give me a break? Work with me? Make life a little more peaceful for me? A life without fear or neglect with stability and safety had been given. That is why she could not understand where I was coming from. I had succeeded in that alone.

My unhealed trauma resulted in me equating her lack of cooperation with how much she loved me, respected me, and appreciated me. All things I should not have been relying on receiving from a child. The typical mother-daughter teen argument would end up being far more intense than it should have been. I wanted her to say what I needed to hear, which was almost impossible because I had brought her up to be strong of mind and opinion. She would not say things just to make me feel better.

When I was triggered by my teen daughter, I felt like she just did not care and was quite happy taking advantage. In the past I had been trodden on, bullied, and abused, because of that I could not accept anyone treating me bad, not even my own teen. This was especially the case because in my eyes, she had a life a million times easier than I had growing up. There was so much conflict and contradiction in me. It was wrong of me to think like this, but I was unaware.

Emotional understanding should never have been expected from a child. My expectations of our relationship had stemmed from my relationship with my mum. That was not a typical relationship. We were extremely close because we were prisoners in the same house.

I am blessed to have realised that I was on my way to creating a trauma team of my own, made up of my own husband and kids and resulting in the second cycle of abuse.

This book is here to help people understand how easy it is to fall into this cycle without realising it. I have lost and won, fallen, and risen, laughed until I peed a little and cried. I have broken and been fixed. I have been stuck in the darkness and clawed my way back towards the light. I have been my own abusive parent, beating myself up, time after time. I have reflected, meditated, and studied everything available. I have seen that there is more to this material world. After all of this, I still nearly fell into the past pain cycle.

I wished someone would have warned me about the seemingly 'normal' things that can creep into your family life that can start downward spirals. It was my manipulation. It was forcing my whole family, my husband, and kids, to be part of a trauma team that they did not consent to be part of. It was manipulating and emotionally blackmailing my family into doing what I needed to keep my mental health good.

These realisations led me to finally listen to my daughter, and when she said again, 'I need to go,' I said 'okay.' My daughter was not running away; she was running towards something. Over the past six years of growing up, she had had no place to run to. No grandma to be spoiled by, no aunties and uncles to go and confide in. No places to seek refuge when things got hard at home. The only place she really had to run to be her bedroom.

It is bittersweet how things work out sometimes. I spent a week coming to terms with the fact that I would have to let her go, which would be way before her eighteenth birthday. I started contemplating letting her go after her sixteenth birthday, which was in three months. I worried about her flying all that way by herself. By the end of that week, unfortunately, things started to fall into place. My husband's grandad passed away, so he would be taking the flight home either way; before I knew it, my husband had a return flight, and my daughter a one way.

THE LETTERS

When my daughter left, I felt the worst anxiety I think I have ever felt before. When I thought about the physical distance between us, I felt sick. My mind convinced me that she felt the same anxiety, and that made me feel extreme. I had minutes where I felt okay about her being away, but those minutes were short.

I had to hold it together for my younger two children. My husband was not there; I did not have the privilege of having him to lean on. My husband would force me to take time to allow myself to break.

Days after my daughter left, I managed to go into her room without crying. I was in her room tidying when I found a notebook containing letters to me and her biological father. The last letter that she wrote was regarding a big argument that we had had before she left.

"Dear mum, I just blew up at you for touching my stuff. I do not know what it is with my stuff that makes me feel the need to blow off. I scratched my arm up badly as punishment for myself. I wish I could go to our home country for a break. To be honest, I just need to figure out what I want and find my worth and fight again. I do love you, and I don't mean anything I say, so please don't take it to heart because you're amazing, and you don't deserve anything but the best. Love you."

"Hey mum, I know I do not write well, but when this book is halfway, I might let you read it anyway. I am going home, and it is going to be okay I promise. I am happy, hurting, and healing all at the same time, and that is also okay. I do not want to be hurting anymore; I need closure. I need, to need you; I am just not feeling connected to anyone anymore. I am not isolating myself, well not on purpose."

"Hey, Dad (biological), four days until I leave now, I'm excited and scared. Mum was stressing about everything, and I get it, but I also don't because she is strong. I've never seen her like this; it's upsetting me and stressing me out, but that's selfish of me. I don't know what to do. At this point, I think I am leaving here, without mum by my side. I wish I were more upset about that possibility, but love is a weakness. I need to learn that It's okay to love and have a normal relationship. I do not even know what I am saying, or where my head is now. Anyway, love you, Goodbye."

"Dear Dad, I am going to be sixteen soon. I never thought I would be without you; I will come and visit your grave. I have not seen it yet. I wish heaven had visiting hours because I miss you so much. I should be home this time next week. I will tell you all about it. Love you"

After reading those words in her notebook I knew my daughter had it all worked out. Every time she had shouted for me to let her go, and I took it personally and said 'no,' she knew that she had work to do that could not be done from here.

When I read about love being a weakness in her diary entry, a light bulb went off in my head. There would only ever be a certain level of closeness and feeling between me and her in case she lost me too. It was self-protection. I felt horrid that the whole time I just thought she did not care.

When I spoke to her and heard the laughter she was bringing to my whole family, I was proud. Her strength and light were shining through. I always tried to remind my daughter that my reactions were never about her. My responses were because her defence mechanism (switching her feelings off) was my trigger. The trigger to let me know that there were unhealed things in me that needed attention.

My daughter had saved me for a second time. She saved me firstly by being born. When she was born, I decided that an abusive relationship might have been good enough for me because that is all I knew, but it was not good enough for my little girl. My daughter gave me the strength to leave that relationship and move on to the next chapter. fifteen years later, her departure would allow me the space to undertake an even deeper dive into my own healing. My daughter's self-awareness was switched on enough to know that she had healing to do that that she could not do here with me. She had to consolidate the death of her father and obtain closure. She had to be away from this family and me to decide who she was, independent of us and independent of me. She had to prove to herself that she could do it. I would never ever have sent her away, I could not but when I heard the laughter and the peace she had found, I knew it was the best thing for the both of us.

Her journey overseas started out as a need to heal and grow, but she ended up gaining far more. I learned so much about myself while she was gone because it was no longer about our relationship. I was able to go deeper into myself, my behaviour, my triggers, and my strength. I was able to see past the everyday annoyances, the expectations, and the fights. I was able to come back to love.

My daughter had times while she was away when she did not feel strong. During these times she held it together because she did not want to upset me. I hated that she did this. I would rather be upset, hear the truth and be able to be there for her. The empathy that my daughter was showing for my feelings had never been displayed by her before. We spoke every day on the phone, both expressing our love for one another by hiding how tight our heartstrings were pulling.

Two weeks before her sixteenth birthday, I gave my daughter her freedom. She had proven far beyond any doubt that she was an independent, critical thinker with massive resilience and her own morals. What more could I ask of a sixteenth-year-old, who had just taken herself halfway around the world to heal from her past pains? Although my daughter struggled, she went to her dad's grave for the first time and made amends with his family.

Giving my daughter her freedom represented me sitting firmly back in my chair. On her return home, I was not going to be on her case about grades at school, careers, or what colour she was dying her hair. There would be support available to her if she needed help with decisions. I would be there to fully support her in those choices, whatever they may be. No longer would I be willing to place on her the expectations that were placed on me.

While we had the space between us, I had been able to write the most painful chapters of this book. When I got to the end of those chapters, I was able to take the only childhood picture I have of myself down from my mirror. I had spent the last year sending love and peace to that little girl and now I felt ready to move on.

UNDERSTANDING HIM

Narrowly missing the recreation of another trauma cycle gave me a much clearer understanding of the mechanics involved in my dad's trauma team. My Dad's mission was to have everyone do as he said, when he said to do it and how he wanted it done. Military-grade perfection was expected in all our actions. If we could achieve these goals, then he believed we would live harmoniously.

Early on in my Mum and Dad's relationship, my dad had all his childhood expectations met. He ran a tight ship, was the boss, the god, everyone obeyed him, and he could do as he pleased. You would think this would be the end of the mission, but it was not. A cycle was still in full swing only now it had to expand, it had to achieve more and encompass more, it needed to prove more. When you are in a trauma cycle and fulfil all your unrealistic expectations, you must create more expectations to keep evaluating your trauma team's (family) compliance, and therefore your control.

He began to push the boundaries of what he could do. Asking even more outlandish and evil things of us, feeding off hurting us in more creative ways. Control became tighter and tighter every year that passed.

My dad, in his justification of himself, had told us that strict expectations were put on him as a child, with severe consequences for not met. Those unmet expectations followed him into adulthood. With his own family, he now creates his trauma team. Each member aiding him to achieve all the childhood expectations put on him. My dad replayed his perceived failures through us, convincing himself he could help us be better. Really, he was trying to make himself better in our successful obedience.

.   I do not excuse my father's actions or any other human being's actions that harm another, but beginning to understand his cycle and, therefore, my cycle was an important part of healing.

HEALING WHILE PARENTING

It is essential that parents or prospective parents, take time to evaluate their patterns, expectations, and assumptions. In an ideal world, we would do this evaluation before we have kids, or at least early on in their lives. This is not an ideal world. We must evaluate which parts of our personality are really ours, and which parts result from external experiences and conditioning. I would suggest yearly self-evaluations. Before you know it, conditioning becomes a habit, which you are then tasked with unlearning. I spent all that summer happily walking around my house, muttering 'not my expectation' as I reviewed various unfinished chores and slightly messy rooms. I am still figuring out precisely what my actual boundaries and expectations are. When I do decide on my expectations, at least I will know they are mine.

Every one of us has only one truth to teach, and that truth is our unique experience of this life. In the following chapters, I will detail the understandings that ushered me through the challenging times and the epiphanies that led me to these understandings. I am of the belief that healing from trauma is a process that encompasses expectation assessment, trigger management, resilience building, and the ability to transmute pain into peace.

I still must remind myself of these factors, and that is ok. Healing is an ongoing process, so as we ride through life, we navigate the bumps a little better than the road before. That is what success looks like for me.

CHAPTER SEVEN

Resilience Building

THE LIFETIME LINE

The very beginning of my active healing journey was about collecting the dots that would eventually be joined. I say 'active' healing because it was the beginning of my conscious choice to heal. I considered all the previous pain, the fighting with myself, to be the most essential part of my healing process, but it was unconscious healing. Without that suffering, there would have been no signposts, that recovery was even needed.

Firstly, a line was drawn on a plain piece of paper. I then wrote my ages, and underneath the age, any key events, positive or negative. The lifetime line was drawn because an overview was needed. To move forward, I would have to first go back.

Lifetime Line

Yrs.	5	10	15	25	30
	First time I became aware of the violence.	We left the flat and had freedom for a few weeks before he found us.	Met my first love and entered my own abusive relationship	23, Gave birth to my daughter.	Met my husband to be.

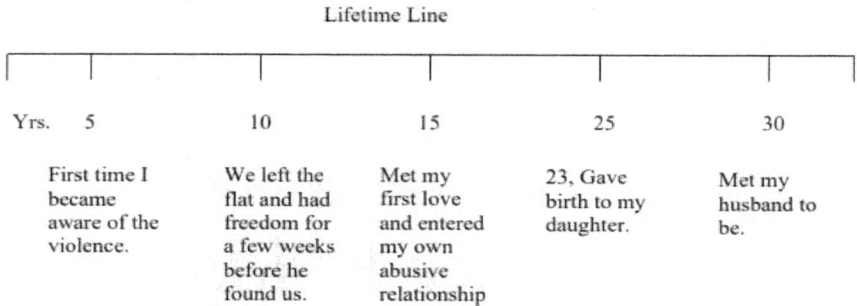

Your lifetime line will have more, or less ages, and a lifetime of detail. The above line is a very small example. As a species, we do not place importance on reflection. We are so consumed with the hustle and bustle of daily life, that we can only ever consider short time spans. If we are lucky, our working minds have access to the past five years and the capability to plan for the next five. We do not have the memory capacity to hold onto things that are deemed unimportant. This is apparent when you factor in the space needed, to process the vast amounts of useless life narration.

Every adult should undertake a lifetime line, or something similar. It is your record of what made you, who you are. There are significant benefits to be found, in sitting down and looking at the bigger picture of you.

I detailed the things that I could remember, on my lifetime line. My next step was to ask my mother a few things, to fill in any gaps. When asking loved ones about sensitive issues, to fill in your memory gaps, use caution. Boxes that cannot be resealed, can be opened. My mother was the only person that could fill in my gaps. I only asked for the dates when we lived in certain houses. That request for information alone, produced more than just dates. It also produced her tears. I would never have dug up the past, had I not been prepared to use that information for the greater good of our family and our cycles. My request was not just out of curiosity.

Once I felt like I had a timeline, I started to study it and look for patterns. I was unsure where I was going with this timeline, but I knew it was needed. The experience of being able to visualise, an overview of my entire life, up until now was very therapeutic. We get so caught up in trying to be better, that we forget what we have already been through, and survived. We forget how far we have come, and the battles already won. I had never looked back before, because life had been busy, filled with fighting. My mind had been scattered, momentarily dipping in and out of the past, and worrying far into the future.

During the completion of my lifetime line, I had failed to be the parent that my eldest daughter needed. Up until my daughter entered her teen years, I had completely dismissed the idea that I had any issues at all. I never acted like someone that needed healing, which meant that there was no evidence to say I did. I was a survivor that prided herself on never using her childhood as an excuse. My lifetime line gave me the first visual glimpse, that the pain that I felt was not a reaction to the situation with my daughter, my hormones, or my challenges. It may be the result of things I had locked away.

CLEARING THE CACHE

Cache definition:

Noun

1. *A collection of items of the same type stored in a hidden or inaccessible place.*

2. *Computing. An auxiliary memory from which high-speed retrieval is possible.*

www.merriam-webster.com

Past pain be it from childhood to past adult pain, leaves us humans, with more than mental scars. Nine times out of ten, it leaves us with an underlying susceptibility to future pain. Why? Because we never truly let go. Suppose you think about how you clean up your computer disk space, delete browsing history from your phone, or clear caches from your smart TV. In that case, these seem like necessary and essential tasks that must be done to make our technology perform better. Why then do we not see the importance of clearing our own hard drives?

Past pain that has not been fully felt, will lie festering on your hard drive, increasing each year of life, causing your computer to run slow. If you do not have any computer knowledge, you start to think this is just how your computer runs. You would eventually (like I did), begin to believe that your computer (mind), is broken or accept that this is the best it is going to get: slow and not very efficient.

It is the same with our minds; if we let past pain build up, it almost becomes who we are; that is how we feel. We feel de-motivated, low energy, and unlucky. If we left nothing behind unresolved, there would be no "things always" or "every time I," sentence starters because the negatives would be deleted, and a fresh start would begin.

It is common knowledge that when we have issues in adult life, those issues are born in our youth, and it does not take a guru to tell us so. Although this is common knowledge, how many people take the time to come out of their mind, map, and extinguish any history that no longer serves them? I read every spiritual/personal development book available to free myself of my mind. I chain watched anything I could on healing, and I still never thought to see if what they said was true. Can I heal my past pain?

It is not an easy or linear path to healing; however, the next step gave me more than enough hope to continue the journey. This simple table, with linked events, provides enough concrete evidence to understand that you are not stuck in an unbreakable loop.

This table works because you see in plain sight how the past and present link up. You realise that you do not have a permanent problem. You just forgot to clear the cache for a long time.

In clearing the cache table, you finally see that although you think you are present, the person you have presented to people has been an outdated version of you. Clearing the cache may not deliver the profound ah-ha moment for everybody, as it did for me. However, what is absolutely guaranteed is that you will feel better positioned to begin dealing with your past pain.

Your issues will no longer be scary, dark, and mysterious things that impact your life. You will have an idea of where they came from and how they were born. Sympathy will be felt for them, because you now know that these issues will not be around forever. Having an idea of where each issue came from means that you can go back, feel, and deal with them.

Depending on the severity of your past pain, the first step will be to have a professional individually assess, whether you need support on your journey. Clearing the cache is a tool to help those people who find it hard to take those first steps.

When you fill out the table below, or recreate a personalised version, note that, it is not important whether the thoughts column comes after, or before the emotion column. There are neuroscientists and psychologists alike, that equally argue in favour of the thought or emotion coming first. Each situation can be different. In my experience, reactionary trigger impulses, start in the body (i.e., someone pushes in front of you in the que). While ongoing triggered states, come through the daily thoughts being created from old systems.

Thoughts were put first in this table because during the beginning of my healing journey most of my emotions were subconscious. I was not able to identify my emotions, without going through my thoughts. My thoughts were loud and obvious and therefore an easier starting point for my healing journey.

Instructions for clearing the cache

(Table A has been done for you to fill in)

1. Refer to table A below.

2. Pull any prominent early life events from the timeline that you created, which caused you pain, be it physical, mental, or emotional, and add it to column **A. Past Pain.**

3. Next, write the main thoughts that came with each of those pains in column **B. Thoughts.**

4. In column **C**, write the main emotions, each thought made you feel.

5. Make a list or pull from the timeline, the main thing/things, at present that cause you pain, be it physical, mental, or emotional, and add to column **D. Current Pain.**

6. In column **E,** write the **main thoughts** that come with each **current pain.**

7. In column **F,** write the **main emotions** that come with each of the **current thoughts.**

8. Go back to column **A. Past Pain** and compare the items to column **F, Current Emotions**. Take time to notice any connections.

9. Go back to column **C. Past Emotions** and compare the items in it to column **E. Current Thoughts**. Take time to notice any connections.

10. Have a lightbulb moment.

Please refer to my table on the following page for an example.

A. Past Pain	B. Past Thoughts	C. Past Emotions	D. Current Pain	E. Current Thoughts	F. Current Emotions
Witnessing violence towards mum as a child.	Why her? Why do good people get hurt? I can't protect her. No one can help us.	Afraid Frustration Helpless Resentful Vulnerable	**Control Unable to be vulnerable. Unable to ask for help.**	I can do it all by myself. I do not need anyone. I must be strong I must predict negative events.	Afraid Frustration Helpless Resentful Vulnerable
My own abusive relationship.	I need him. I am not good enough for him. I have nothing. Maybe it is my fault he hurts me. When will he hurt me next?	Hopeless Worthless Belittled Scared Sad	**Triggered Anger Low Self Worth The need for Validation Fear of being treated bad. Fear of failing.**	I do not need anyone. I deserve respect. If they loved me, they would…	Hopeless Worthless Belittled Scared Sad

Table A

142

A. Past Pain	B. Past Thoughts	C. Past Emotions	D. Current Pain	E. Current Thoughts	F. Current Emotions

Table B

My Observations

Despite the number of years that had gone by, no matter how new, and surprising problems felt, it was all based on old past energy.

9. Go back to column C. Past Emotions and compare the items in it to column E. Current Thoughts. Take time to notice any connections

C. Past Emotions	E. Current Thoughts
Afraid Frustration Helpless Resentful Vulnerable	I can do it all by myself. I do not need anyone. I must be strong I must predict negative events.
Hopeless Worthless Belittled Scared Sad	I do not need anyone. I deserve respect. If they loved me, they would…

Table C

I found that my current thoughts and current problems link directly back to the first negative emotions and the first past pains. I also noticed that my current thoughts, although opposite to the original emotions clearly shared the same energy and relationship.

144

For Example, I felt fear during my past pain. As I grew up, this fear manifested itself as the attitude 'I am the boss.'

When trying to grow a family, being a control freak brings problems.

For Example, I felt let down during my past pain; this feeling manifested in my 'I don't need anyone' attitude.

These attitudes are seen as positive in current society. However, the latter attitude, resulted in me constructing a wall of defence, that even my husband could not penetrate. There is a difference between not needing people and being unable to let people in, even if you wanted to.

My past emotions, create my current thought system. This thought system, is based on opposition and survival. My current thought system subconsciously creates new pains, and challenges, to justify the lingering presence of the past pain emotions. The emotions live in the hope of one day being acknowledged in their original state and therefor released.

Hopefully, you may notice other links of which you were not aware. Either way it is a wonderful thing, to realise that things are not always just happening to us, we are not at the mercy of a random and chaotic world.

PERIODS AND PERSPECTIVES

Before I understood my underlying issues, I thought my problems were based on my hormones; biology was to blame. My period was my initial trigger. It was the first issue that made me think about looking for answers. This first issue gave birth to my understanding that anything can be changed.

The first point of call was to visit the doctors to have hormone tests. By this point, I was already eating healthier and was going to the gym. My health, in general, was better than it had ever been. I was learning about holistic medicine, so the thought of potentially needing pharmaceuticals to balance my hormones was not a positive experience. I went to the doctors and took the hormone test, fully expecting a significant imbalance that would more than likely need medicating. The test came back completely normal; I was shocked.

Plan A was crumbling. There was no biological reason for me to act and feel like a foreigner in my own life, for two weeks out of every single month. The situation was wearing me down. I needed my energy to parent my two younger kids and navigate mine and my eldest daughter's relationship.

With an open mind and a hint of desperation, the research into menstruation began. The only expectation I had was that it would be biological information that would be found. At this point, anything would help. I came across two exciting things.

The first thing was found while reading about the history of menstruation in diverse cultures. I was shocked to find that although ancient cultures were confused and scared about the meaning of a woman's menstruation, some placed an extremely high regard on the time.

This high regard was seen in the red tents of the Native Americans. When it was time for the women of the tribe to menstruate, they would go off to a red tent; during this time, they would meditate, dream, and relax. When the women's periods were over, they would return to the tribe. The tribe members would question the women about their dreams, and the women would tell of predictions they had seen within their dreams. These predictions included information on moving their camps, natural resource availability, or the foretelling of coming droughts The men of the tribe would take these dreams very seriously. It was believed that when a woman was menstruating, her connexion to source/God/universal knowledge was extremely strong.

This information blew my mind. How had I never heard this information? How were we not taught this cultural perspective in school as teenagers? Instead, we were left with a negative view of our periods, as though they were our punishments. As young women, how often did we declare that we wished we were not female all because of our perceived negative periods? Not only were we not offered any positive perspectives or images of menstruation, but we also had the negative narratives of modern periods encouraged.

Society told us that our menstruation was the only time we were allowed to be angry and act out of character; furthermore, it was expected. Movies and media all carried stereotypical images and phrases. When a woman decided to speak her mind or show her unhappiness, "are you on your period?" became an insult instead of a question. It could only be the fault of evil hormones as to why we act out (aka showing our true feelings/state of mind).

With these negative generational connotations in mind, we use our periods to release all the pent-up frustrations and emotions that we did not allow ourselves to communicate. This cycle made our menstruations morph into something we dreaded.

When your period has the subconscious purpose of releasing past pain or trauma, it will be physically more painful. When we use the excuse of our period to fight and demand our worth, as in my case, we give up our authentic power and hand it over to a fake concept. Painful periods are also experienced when our souls are worn out. As women, we do it all, and all the time. Never allowing ourselves time off. When our energy begins to stay at a low level, nature forces us to rest by providing physical pain or illness. When you no longer need your period to provide an outlet, it becomes almost insignificant as mine eventually did.

There is no exaggeration to say that I was a nightmare to live with for two whole weeks of every month. Add in the unhealed trauma lying dormant within me, waiting for an opportunity to seep into life, and you have a ticking time bomb. After reading about the Red Tents, my period instantaneously changed. The more I read and understood the spiritual nature of menstruation, the more my period took on a different meaning. I found out that a woman's period was not only a time for the release of biological elements, but the release of anything from that past month that no longer served your higher purpose. It was a time of reflection and outstanding insight.

It is funny how finding the words to match your experience validates the experience and brings it into life and out of your head.

When I read about the dreams, I instantly remembered that my dreams were more vivid just before I was due to come on my period. It all made sense. This information that I had absorbed resonated with me completely. The information that resonated with me may not be for you. The words may not perfectly explain the feelings that you thought were indescribable. However, if you search, you will find those that flip the negative in your life on its head, creating something positive. The point is to look.

My period is now 100% better. I have no symptoms, no dramatic emotions, and no pain apart from day one. The day one pain is not even enough to take a paracetamol. A significant shift was immediate, but the growth that came with it was ongoing. This event sparked the change in how I saw myself as a woman and the understanding that this world contains different views, stories, and perspectives, all of which I could use. I could choose the ones that suited me and my life instead of just accepting the perspective given/handed down to me. Do you want new? Do you want to change? The tools are out there, but you must go and seek them out.

I have included this anecdote about my period because perspective has been a powerful tool for coping with life. The superpower of perspective got me through my painful childhood. Perspective helped when my daughter's father passed away and helped me deal with that grief. Perspective is a surprising, unexpected solution to the problem that you cannot find the answer to. In perspective lies a new set of eyes. With those new eyes come new ways of looking at the problem and new ways of understanding. Sometimes when we are drowning in ourselves, a unique perspective can be the hand of a stranger that pulls us out.

Perspective helps us to be open to more than just our own view on a situation. We cannot see the bigger picture of our lives within society, so the ability to seek out different perspectives on a problem, is an effective tool for personal development.

Another good example of when perspective was used is in our finances. With only one wage to live on, due to prioritising raising our kids, meant that things sometimes got tough. A big, unexpected bill, and we would feel the pinch. I would put myself under huge unnecessary stress during these times as it helped me release trauma energy.

This undue stress had a purpose. The purpose was to relieve me of a feeling I constantly carried in my stomach. It was the feeling that something terrible was going to happen. No matter how peaceful life was, the sucker punch to my gut was indeed on its way.

Having a stressful event like financial strain gave me peace in a weird way. I had a break from the waiting and was able to see the unpleasant event that had been on its way. Once the financial strain had subsided, which it always did, I was back in fight or flight mode, waiting for the punch.

When you begin to do the work and address your pain, you no longer need to use current situations as ways to release all that you bottle up. Through perspective, I became conscious of my use of outside events to release pain. I was able to see financial strain differently. There was a positivity to be found in the financial stress. I looked at it from an unfamiliar perspective. I decided that yes, sometimes things got tight but, we were able to pay those unexpected expenses. I asked myself questions and answered honestly. I asked myself, *would I go back and change my decision to focus on the kids during their early years and instead go out to work?* The answer was always no, no matter how frustrated I felt.

The power of perspective enables us to take positives from painful situations. For me being able to use the power of perspective was empowering. It meant that no matter how bad the situation, I could bend it into something that I could manage. I could create a choice where there was none. Using perspective is not to justify a person's hurtful or abusive behaviour towards you. Perspective does not take problems away, but it does make them more manageable, therefore freeing up thinking space for finding solutions.

MICRO TRIGGER STACKING

While we are busy working on what we think are the significant issues, we should be aware of letting the 'small' things build up. Stacking, I noticed, was an unnecessary problem. While working on myself, I would have times when progress was being made. Every so often, I would blow up over something small. I would beat myself up as usual and take the slip up as a sign that I was not actually making progress.

After reflection, I realised that the blow-ups over the 'small' things resulted from my unconscious stacking of micro-triggers. Micro triggers are the things that do not warrant massive reactions. They are the minor annoyances that are not worthy of your full fight. The problem is that these little micro triggers, when left unattended, can stack up. They keep stacking until the tower is big enough to topple. Micro triggers can have their own individual piles. There can be a general stack of life's complaints. There can also be person-based stacks; every time a particular person does something you do not like; another chip goes on the pile. It might be a feeling type stack, i.e., 'unappreciation,' whenever someone does not say thank you or return favours, a micro-trigger chip goes on the stack. While the stacks are small, there are no massive reactions, feelings are still there, only on a much smaller scale.

As we travel along our healing, there will always be bumps in the road. The most painful bumps in the road for me, were during extended periods of peace. There would be an overreaction and it would seem like suddenly; I had let myself be unnecessarily triggered. The pain of moving so far forward, only to be triggered by something small, felt worse than the pain was before any healing had occurred. It felt like I had failed during these times, and it hurt. There was no failure, just the last chip on the stack. The minor issues had grown without my attention and evolved into something with the power to blow.

To keep my peace for longer, I now try and deal with each trigger chip as it comes. I express how I feel, but without expecting the other person to understand or feel the same way as I do. It is about feeling the emotions and communicating them that releases the chip

CHAPTER EIGHT

Expectation Assessment

WHERE DO THEY COME FROM?

The word expectation never really crossed my mind during life. This is bizarre because it turned out to be that which my challenges, were based on. The word 'expectation' was clearly influential; however, the process of its development was invisible to the naked eye. My life was spent rolling with the punches, winning fights, and then waiting for the next. I could only see the small picture, and I certainly could not join any dots. This fog would last into my thirties. I felt secure in my personality, really, I was a stranger to myself.

Expectations are predictions that we make about the future; these predictions are based on the past. We think or say things like, 'every time I try to...........happens,' or '...............always works out for me.'

Expectations can also be born in the present. These expectations are the children of our egos. These expectations say things like 'I just did something for you, now you will be nice to me.'

Despite my history of trauma, I knew what was real and what was not. How could I have been so sure of this statement when the only reference points I had was a horrendous childhood and violent young adulthood.

You could say our expectation is nothing more than a sign that our brains are in good working order, sound predictions require thought and reflection. The problem is, we rarely put thought into our expectations, neither why we have them nor where they came from.

Expectations come from a broad array of areas in life. Our first expectations are simple, as babies, we feel unfulfilled in our bodies and cry. From this, we expect to be provided with milk as we doze back off, engulfed in the warm, fuzzy, full feeling. When we are children, if all has gone well, we can expect a parent to race over and kiss our knees better after a fall. We could have expected to be tucked in at night and read our favourite story. We could have expected to be softly awoken in the morning, safe in the knowledge that we were loved.

Not all children were raised with the same expectations. Some children learned that they could not make their parents love them no matter how hard they tried. Some children knew that the only way to survive was by predicting every moment and expecting the worst. Some children learned that they were a burden, and because of that, they were in debt just for being alive. Some like me knew not to expect to be saved.

As adults, these children expect pain and heartache. They live behind walls of false strength and independence. These children learned not to expect anyone to come. As adults like me, these kids lived in suspended fear. No matter how good life is, you are always waiting for that sucker punch in your stomach, the moment that you realize the holiday is over. We learn what to expect from our parents or lack of firstly, we learn what to expect from relationships and ourselves. The expectations that we learn from our parents can either be taken on board consciously or subconsciously. We consciously take on the expectations that we deem of a positive nature; these are the expectations that we see being met, and result in a form of gratification (pleasure).

For example, we may see our mothers expect to be helped by our father, we may see our father help her, we then see our mothers show our father gratitude and the balance of harmony.

On the other hand, if your mother expected your father to help her, and this expectation was continuously not met, the result observed would be frustrations, disagreements, and arguments.

In the last example, if you were exposed to this situation for an extended period, you would go into adulthood, not expecting a partner to help or support you. As a child, you would not consciously take the latter example on board for future reference. However, subconsciously, the seed would be sown.

The future adult in this second scenario may develop and accept the belief that you cannot expect help from a partner. This would cause problems, such as not communicating that you need help, because you assume that they will not help anyway. The future adult in the second scenario, may also develop opposing expectations. Such as '*I will never end up like my mum'*, based on rejection of outcomes, observed as a child.

I vowed to never allow a man to treat me how my dad had treated her, not in a million years. This is problematic because we cannot accurately predict other people's behaviour. By sixteen-years- old, I was already in an abusive relationship. My firm belief in my expectations (I would never end up like my mum) was the reason I found it so hard to admit the situation that I was in.

The society we live in also plays a significant role in creating our expectations; society is like our extended family. With the help of the media, society dictates what our expectations should be, at any given time based on its need to survive. Unrealistic expectations are put in place by society when we are children; straight away, we are set up for a fall.

Disney tried to convince all the little girls that a Prince Charming would come and save us. I was one of those little girls. I knew, in reality, no one was coming, but in my dream world as a teenager, I would meet a tall, handsome stranger, who would whisk me away from the life I was living. The power of this ideology alone is enormously underestimated. Imagine convincing generations of women that they had no personal power? Imagine convincing little girls in unspeakable situations that girls do get saved, but not you. Imagine selling the dream to the millions of children worldwide that the bad guys lose in the end, while those kids continue, year by year fighting to survive.

It suited society at the time to promote the happy ever after. It also served society to portray the male as the rescuer.

Fast forward to today's Disney movies, and we have strong female leads, which is fantastic, but worryingly there is always a missing parent that has either died or left. This observation led me to ask 'is the media reflecting or perpetuating society? My kids understand different family structures because I have taught them. Still, they are confused as to why every kid's movie has an absent parent.

There is no doubt there are more one-parent families than ever before. How much of the conditioning the kids receive, will influence their future expectations of what a family should look like? One parent homes that love and provide for their children, while overcoming sometimes impossible challenges, do excellent jobs of raising their kids. The truth is however, it is still easier to raise a family with the help of a supportive partner. If that is the truth, should we be conditioning kids that the norm is a one-parent family?

The point here is that expectations are built over different platforms, times and are dependent on many variables. The biggest natural platform for expectation creation is lived experience; the biggest manufactured platform is the media. If a large chunk of our expectations are learned, how can we automatically base our lives on them?

THE 'QUEEN' CONUNDRUM

Confusion has arisen from the mixed messages delivered to us females. We are told to have ambitious standards and to demand to be treated a certain way. We see stories, so-called reality shows, influencers old and young, detailing perfect lives. We then look at the people in our own lives and wonder why they do not treat us how everyone else is being treated.

The social media machine churns out standards, of what constitutes love and appreciation. The whole 'we are all queens' trend, reinforces unrealistic expectations of life and other human beings.

If we look at the concept of a queen, what words or images would spring to mind? Traditionally we would see power, control, an abundance of materialism, and respect. If your life mission is to gain power, riches, and respect, then yes, becoming a queen figuratively speaking, would be the path to take. To convince us that we are all queens in such a sweeping way is worrisome.

We are not all queens. We do not have riches or a land portfolio, and we have little to no authority in society. Are we all queens metaphorically? That depends on what your idea of a metaphorical queen would be. For me, if I had to use that word, a queen would be described as someone who has been through battles and comes back to get her people; she is someone who stands for something, someone who has seen her own dark days and returned with the light. A queen realizes when there is work to be done.

The acknowledgement that we all have work to do on ourselves, provides us with humility and compassion, for other human beings on their own unique journeys. A queen is someone who lives her life intentionally, regardless of all the other external factors and expectations.

The queen propaganda would have made, more of a lasting impact, had it focused on the standards we hold ourselves to, instead of our expectations of external concepts and other people. With the help of the media, we have convinced ourselves, that we have the right to have our expectations of other people met. We are taught to expect to be treated like a queen, yet most do not even treat themselves like queens. This is not our fault. We have just been taught the wrong priorities.

We all expected that we would find our other half and be completed. These partners would treat us like the queens we are, then we would finally believe in our own worth. Real growth does not work this way, as we learn through experience repeatedly. True self-worth comes from us first and is not reliant on a second opinion.

Questions

1. What Expectations of other people do you currently hold? Number them in a list on a piece of paper.
2. For each expectation, think about why you have it, and write it down.
3. Next to each expectation, write how you feel about yourself when this expectation is not met.

4. Lastly, for each expectation, write those to whom you think it originally belongs.

The following page details my answers to these questions that I asked myself.

1. What Expectations of other people do you currently hold? Number them in a list on a piece of paper
   a. My kids should respect me.
   b. I should be appreciated.
   c. I should be seen to be a good mother.
   d. Everything around me should be kept in order.

2. For each expectation, think about why you have it and write it down
   a. I was taught this.
   b. My mother was not appreciated.
   c. I want to be the opposite of my dad.
   d. I was taught this.

3. Next to each expectation, write how you feel about yourself when this expectation is not met.
   a. I have failed to teach them correctly.
   b. I am being taken advantage of again.
   c. I am failing as a mother.
   d. The people around me do not love me enough to do the things I need them to do.

4. Lastly, for each expectation, write those to whom it originally belongs.
   a. My dad's.
   b. Mine- born from wanting to be the opposite of what I learned as a kid.
   c. Mine-born from needing reassurance that I am doing ok as a mother.
   d. My dad's.

You can see here that my expectations were either not mine or were born wanting the opposite of what I had witnessed.

WHO DO WE THINK WE ARE?

After demanding to be treated a particular way unsuccessfully, we then throw tantrums because those demands are not met. We cry out tears of pain when someone we care about refuses to change. Confused anger washes over us when someone does not present the feelings that we logically (or socially) think they should. A person's love for us is put into question when the other person cannot say the words we need to hear. We become bound in the frustration caused by repeatedly explaining what we need and how we need it, to no avail.

We observe the people in our lives like a teacher assessing a student; every time there is an opportunity to evaluate them, we do. *Did they listen to me the last time I explained? Will they do better? Will they fail again?* This need, to correct other people, comes from a strong belief held by all of us. We believe that we all think the same way. And for those that think differently, they just take persuasion.

This could not be further from the truth. In our minds, we live in entirely different worlds. We see the world through custom made lenses that fit only us. No person on this earth has had the exact identical life and experience as another. This means that every person has a different reference point. Humans can observe the same event and give completely opposing accounts of what happened. How then do we have the right to expect someone, (as I did with my daughter), to not only think the same way we do, but also feel how we expect them to feel?

Whether you believe in God, the universe, the dependable simplicity of nature, or the spark of life that starts a baby's heart beating, you know that there is something within us that is miraculous. Inside of us is an energy that cannot be destroyed. It is scientifically proven that energy can only be changed into something else. It can never die; it is infinite in nature. Every energetic soul on this earth has its own path to live, its own pain to transcend, and its own challenges to overcome.

If this is so, then who are we to impose our own tests and challenges? Who are we to engage with someone as though we are the teacher? As though we know best. We are not Gods, over each other, and we do not have the right to say what someone should be learning in this lifetime.

For example, if a man wants a relationship to be successful, then that may be enough motivation for him to work on communication, but then again, it might not.

It is not for me to tell my partner that he needs to communicate better. I can tell my partner that I am finding it difficult to gauge how he is feeling. I can also tell him that I am struggling to understand what he is trying to communicate to me. In the end, it is his job as a living breathing soul to figure out his own challenges and do the work.

I do not have the right to emotionally blackmail him because the relationship is not enough motivation for him to improve his communication skills. People have the right to come to their own realization. If, by chance, advice alone is enough, they may miss a significant step in the process of self and soul development.

For example, I guilt-tripped my daughter because I could not understand why my very visual frustration and upset, was not enough motivation for her to conform and be the person I needed her to be.

Do not think that I am expressing that we should accept hurtful, abusive, or selfish behaviour from a partner, friend, or family member. That is not the case. What I wish to do is deliver another perspective. Understanding why my expectations were both unrealistic and depowering was the most enlightening thing that I did.

What is the alternative to expecting from others? Easy, we expect from ourselves instead. Before we can expect from ourselves, we need to assess the expectations we already have. Once we know which ones do not belong to us, we can begin setting new realistic expectations. Expectations are more practical when we can better control the outcomes. We can better manage the results when expectations are based on our own behaviour.

Let us look at a common expectation we may have of another person. "I expect my partner to respect my time."

For example, *you have not had adequate time to spend with your partner all week, you are super excited as a window of free time has come up.*

You both get together, and very quickly, he/she is on his/her phone scrolling.

This can go wrong. There are so many uncontrollable variables in this scenario, that it should be almost impossible to assume anything, but we do. In my expectation of my partner, I am assuming unrightfully the following different things:

1. That I even know what him valuing my time looks like.
2. That he does value my time.
3. That he can communicate the concept of valuing my time.
4. He has a reference point of what it looks like when you value someone's time.
5. Time is an important commodity to him.

Many of us have expectations that make it easy to write someone off as being wrong, not loving you, or not wanting to make you happy. These assumptions do not account for the individuality of a human mind or the of their individual experience.

The previous scenario could have played out for months or even years. There is no need for the pain and frustration contained in this battle. The battle to make my partner change would have involved me using various conscious and unconscious tactics. This battle would cost countless energy on both sides. I would show him how angry his lack of respect for my time makes me. Eventually, my anger would become sorrow (or vice versa), and tears of frustration would flow. If neither of these exhibitions of emotions moved my partner to change, I would begin to mirror his behaviour. Mirroring his behaviour would make me feel bitter because I now must act out of character.

The above example of an expectation of my partner is expressed below as an expectation of myself:

"I will not go where my energy does not flow."

This would be a very solid, stable expectation of myself. This expectation would mean that I would not put myself in or remain in a situation where I did not feel the flow of energy between me and that person.

Energy flow between people is the process of energy leaving one person that is giving, that energy being received by the other person, who then sends energy back to you. It is the ebb and flow cycle that is found in our interactions with other people. You do not have to be 'new age spiritual' or an expert in meditation, to feel when your energy is going nowhere.

Having expectations of ourselves instead of other people, takes back the only absolute control we have which is over ourselves. To enforce our expectations of ourselves, we have boundaries. Boundaries are like alarmed fences. They signal that our expectations of ourselves need attention.

BOUNDARY BREACHES

A boundary breach for the self-expectation 'I will only go where my energy flows' might look like a friend turning up late for a lunch date and providing no acknowledgment. It is up to me how many boundary breaches are to be accepted from that same friend. One thing that would make this situation different with self-expectations as opposed to people's expectations would be that there should be little to no drama. This is not to say that there would be no feelings about this situation. In the event of being stood up, I would feel worried and disappointed.

The scenario may happen repeatedly. Moving on from the moment it happened, I would be able to quickly resume my everyday life. I would not be angry. I would not spend days, weeks, or months creating negative energy, going over what had happened, and then another few weeks guessing why. I would have to leave it be, simply because I cannot see inside her head. Even if the friend explained why the situation was being repeated, I still would not know if I had all the information needed to accurately assess the problem.

Expecting of myself instead of her, not only respects her as an individual soul, who may have more than I know going on in her life, but it also empowers me. Expecting of myself means my self-worth and happiness is not dependent on her understanding, realizing, or following the same codes of conduct as me. All I would really know for sure in that scenario, would be that she had breached the boundary of my expectation 'I will only go where my energy flows,' and she has done it multiple times. It would now be up to me to decide how to move forward. Do I give it another go? Or do I start to back off from that situation? Either way, it is on me, not her.

Expectations are so important because of the potential result of not having them met; triggers.

CHAPTER NINE

❦

Trigger Management

WHAT ARE TRIGGERS?

Definition of the word trigger

noun

1. A small device that releases a spring or catch and so sets off a mechanism, especially to fire a gun.

verb

1. Cause (a device) to function.

In Psychology, the term 'triggered' indicates a stimulus such as a sound, a smell, or a sight that triggers feelings of trauma. An article on the guardian.com website titled 'trigger warning: how did 'triggered' come to mean upset'? describes the original word 'trigger' as denoting the lever of a gun or a trap. It states that the word's original spelling was 'tricker,' which was taken from the Dutch word 'trekken' meaning to pull. Had I been asked to link the word to trigger a force, i.e., pull, push, I would have linked it with 'push.' The force 'push' would come to mind because when triggered, there would be a sense of being pushed towards a particular reaction, and one that was unwanted.

After gaining insight into the purpose of triggers, the original meaning, and the force 'to pull' made more sense. When I get triggered now, the triggers are pulling reactions out of me that are sometimes buried deep in my subconscious. Triggers are there to pull out of us that which needs attention. We all have both positive and negative triggers, with varying intensities, based on how they are stored as memories.

Triggers may be obvious, for example, the death of a family pet being triggered by the sight of a similar-looking animal. Triggers may not be so obvious, like anger arising when someone is treating you nicely. Triggers speak through emotions, and emotions are born in the body. Emotions are the body's reactions to lived or imagined experiences and met or unmet expectations. Therefore, triggers are born first in our bodies.

For example, someone pushes in front of me in a queue, when I am in a rush, my heart starts to beat fast, and my muscles begin to tense. My mind decodes this physical communication as anger. After my mind decodes the body signals, thoughts cross my mind to justify the feeling, e.g., *this guy is taking advantage.'* The queue jumper inadvertently triggered a memory, and now I am feeling belittled.

MAP MY MEMORY

Imagine for a minute, going out for a relaxed jog, you decide on a route you have never been before. You set out full of energy and hope for a very scenic experience. You log in to your preferred app of choice, which will track your location, speed, and the distance you have travelled. In the app, you can also document the jog with pictures and feedback. You have been jogging for fifteen minutes when you come to a lovely duck pond. You pause the run and go towards a group of ducks that are gathered, to take a photo.

As you get closer, you realise the ducks are gathered around a baby duck. The baby duck has been bit by something and is no longer alive. You are sensitive to animals, so you pick the baby duck up with leaves and tuck it away in a bush. It is not a pleasant experience. As you start to jog off, you feel upset and deflated, tears start rolling down your face. You keep jogging because you just want to get home. You get more upset and run faster and faster. As you are sprinting, you fall over and scrape your leg. You limp home and stop for the day.

The map created on your run is like a memory in our minds. Along any experience route, there are smells, sounds, pictures, locations, and feelings. As we age, we have less memory space and will not retain every experience. We only include those memories of significance. Either because they are a uniquely positive experience or a negative experience that has not been fully released yet.

The baby duck incident triggered a memory map that was suppressed. When the runner was a child growing up, her mother was very controlling and aggressive. When her mother would drink alcohol, she would get mad and kick the family dog until it cried. As a child watching this happen, she would feel devastated and helpless. The dead duckling situation triggered the emotions that were still trapped within her from childhood. The feelings were still there because the memory map was still relevant. The jogger had not spent any time going back and making peace with her experiences as a child.

Despite not being a fan of continuously living in the past or the future, I believe a trip back can really benefit us moving forward. There is no need for an in-depth analysis of negative experiences; sometimes, all that is needed is to apply the knowledge gained as adults, to the situations we could not understand as children and young people. As adults, we have better understandings of cycles and the environment.

If the jogger were to revisit her painful childhood, she might see behind the circumstance. The jogger may notice the cycles or unaddressed trauma that her own mother had gone through. She may see that her mother's past pain manifested emotionally in her anger and physically in the pain that she habitually inflicted on the family dog.

The jogger may have suffered feelings of inadequacy in her adult life because she could not stop certain situations from happening as a child. Years may have been spent enduring a strained relationship with her mother; she may have wondered why her mum would let her feel unloved by her actions. Memories would include pleading with her mother to calm down and then curling up in a ball sobbing, holding her injured dog.

Going back to really understand what that period of her life was about would not be to justify the mother's behaviour. The journey back would enable the jogger to realise that her mother's behaviour was never a personal attack on her. It would also help her see that her mother's lack of compassion for her as a child was never a reflection of the daughter's self-worth. The mother's behaviour was only a reflection of her own unhealed and ignored pain.

A trigger can act as a catalyst. Depending on how we manage those triggers, they have the potential to become catalysts for positive development. Triggers have an unnecessarily bad reputation; they can guide our healing in beautiful ways. To use these triggers, we must address the old conditioning surrounding emotions and feelings. The way we process emotions and feelings in the past will not serve us in the future, and it is not helping us now. Suppressing emotional pain does just that. It hides it. It does not get rid of it. Just because you are not acknowledging it does not mean it is not there. It remains in our souls and manifests in our bodies as illness or dis-ease.

To use our triggers positively, we must practice being honest with ourselves, enough to explore what our triggers are trying to tell us. We need to stop beating ourselves up for being human and feeling. How can we be wrong for being sad and shedding tears about something that broke our hearts? How can we be made to feel bad for breaking under the pressure when life is too much?

Triggers are messages that bring the miracle of insight into our lives. They make us aware that we were not living as the best versions of ourselves, our true selves. Without triggers, we would just accept our problems as being part of who we are.

Once you have made peace with a painful memory map, it becomes archived and is not so readily available at the slight of a trigger. Eventually, the memory gets pushed out of the space with new experiences and information.

FIGHTING MYSELF

In my experience, which is the only thing I can talk about with any authority, triggers are not born from the trauma alone, but the expectations derived from the experience. My triggers came from my unmet expectations, my expectations came from my conditioning, and my conditioning came first from my childhood.

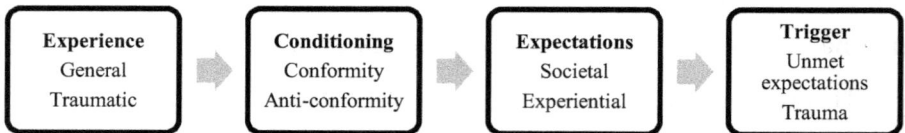

Experience General Traumatic	→	**Conditioning** Conformity Anti-conformity	→	**Expectations** Societal Experiential	→	**Trigger** Unmet expectations Trauma

For example:

Experience: Volatile childhood
Conditioning: Peace does not last
Expectation: Something bad
Trigger: Periods of peace

After learning about my expectations, delving deep into which ones were mine and which were not, I still encountered challenges. Even though I had begun to expect of myself instead of expecting from my eldest daughter, I was still being triggered. My pain was still being activated. This time however it was because my expectations of myself were not being met.

In my triggered state, I resorted to self-punishment. I would mentally beat myself up, draining my own energy in fits of frustration and tears, crumbling in defeat. This behaviour, although depleting, was less painful than expecting my eldest daughter. The pain experienced from expecting from my daughter was threefold. I suffered pain in thinking that my daughter did not care that her behaviour triggered me. I was then triggered by myself for expecting a teenager to help me not to be triggered. Then I was triggered because I felt like I was taking ten steps forward then eleven steps back.

I should have been far kinder to myself during the transition into expecting of myself instead of other people. I should have been aware that it was going to be a journey. Unfortunately, we have grown up in a society that chastises us for being or acting like human beings. The world, for many people, is a terrible place haunted by the ghosts of past pain. So many things happen to us early on in life, but those things do not receive the benefit of our focused attention and care. They become locked away, suppressed, and denied until something or someone in our future triggers us into remembering. When we do not understand that we are being triggered, we believe our extreme reactions are who we are.

175

We end up in frustration wanting to disown ourselves. In the depth of my despair, I wanted to give up being me.

THE EGO

By the time I was ready to address my triggers, I knew that what was being triggered was not my soul self but my personality. It was my inner persona, my ego. The word 'ego' comes from the Latin word for 'I' as in 'I love you' The word ego is most linked to the work of Sigmund Freud, who referred to the 'I' in his works; this 'I' was later translated to 'ego.' In Freudian psychology, the ego or the 'I" mediates between the self-serving 'Id' or the child in us and the morally sensitive 'Superego' the suppressing parent. According to Freudian psychology, the ego keeps everything in balance but can sometimes sway one way or another depending on the cases put forward by the 'ID' and the 'Superego.'

What is funny about the ego's apparent desire for harmony is that popular concepts portray the opposite of balance. As I was growing up and even as a young adult, the only time I would really come across the word ego or any imagery surrounding the word would be concerning either a character on the TV or a description of a person in real life. The character on TV would be an exaggerated example of what I would see in the real-life character of someone described using the word ego.

The person on the TV would have an over-inflated view of themselves with an overflowing abundance of self-confidence. The TV character would disregard other people's wants and needs and be classified as selfish. This person in real life would be called egotistical. We would say that the person has a massive ego, but what would we mean by that? It would mean a similar personality type as the character on the TV. Differences in real life would be in the intensity. It may need watering down to fit in society. An overinflated ego may need to be more undercover in revealing that part of its personality in real life. In the real, world people would react to this person with distaste and discomfort, because it is not cool to be all about yourself.

The world we live in not only convinces us not to put ourselves first but also that showing pain and emotion is weak. We have been convinced that to be successful, we should always present a strong face. Society hijacked the word ego and used it to make us feel bad for wanting better for ourselves. To meet and be in our egos brings natural healing. In our egos, we realise that we must concentrate on ourselves first, not in a selfish way but logically. How can I help someone else or have an authentic view of life without accessing old judgements, beliefs, and programming? The encouraged lack of self-awareness and reflection left us as an individual and social, boiling pot of unresolved pain.

After reading various books, I wrongly concluded that the whole point of personal development and evolvement was to completely get rid of the ego. I decided that the ego was this shadowy, dark, opposing force that tries to trick us into feeling things we do not really feel. That was partly true for me. However, a big part of the ego's purpose was missing.

Early on in my healing journey, after my New Year's Eve breakdown due to throwing my eldest out of my house, I began to really monitor my thoughts. After months of watching my thoughts, I observed that most were either, repetitive life commentaries or my ego trying to protect me. That was a breakthrough for me. The fact that I could watch my own thoughts was a momentous change. The guru Mooji, in one of his Satsang's pointed out that if you can observe your thoughts, then they are not you. You are the one that is watching them.

 This breakthrough sparked the beginning of the separation between myself and the hundreds of ridiculous thoughts I would have in a day. One of those days stuck in my mind. I had begun looking at my body and its health and was making slight changes in what I was consuming and my fitness levels. I joined a gym and had been going for a few months; one day, as I got on the treadmill and began to run, I noticed something strange. There was a young girl at the side of me, also on a treadmill. The girl looked new to the gym, or the machine as she fumbled around the buttons.

I began to run, and as I ran harder and faster, I started to speak for the girl beside me in my own mind. She said, 'wow, she is fast, she must be fit.' As soon as this thought radiated out of my mind, I was in shock and confused. Why had I just taken it upon myself to think for a whole other human being? At this point in my journey, I had not even scratched the surface of my spirituality, let alone be in the position to think I was psychic.

I laughed at myself. I felt ridiculous, and rightfully so. In the end, was the realisation that a pat on the back was needed. I needed to be told that I was doing an excellent job. Why could I not just tell myself? Why in that instance was I unable to just say,' do you know what, we are doing great and give myself a tap on the back? Why was my need for external praise so strong that I was willing to pretend that I knew what someone else was thinking? The answer is that we have been wrongly taught that everything we need is on the outside of us, meaning that we cannot rely on ourselves.

We have been taught not to trust ourselves to the point that someone else must validate what we think for it to be true.

THE FIRST RESPONDER

There are various theories and perspectives on the ego, regarding how it is created, maintained and whether it is beneficial or detrimental. I have enjoyed reading all of them. When I discuss the ego, it is personal experience-based; this is the only way I can speak on it accurately. I hope that in explaining the ego through my own experience, someone somewhere can relate.

I had always been proud to be a thinker; there was pride in my logical and rational mind. My mind was my best friend and my biggest enemy. The fact that I could now listen to it, observe it, and see it continue autopilot made me realise that I was not at war with myself, but an entity powered by the past. There was a missing piece of information that I did not find in any of the books that I read.

The missing information was that before you can defeat something or remove it, in this case, the ego, you must build a relationship and understand it. At first, I was at war with my ego. It was hard to begin to build a relationship with it, because there was also all the noise of the constant life narration. I could not determine which noise was me and which was my ego. The observation of my thoughts continued for months. It was like a parent watching their mischievous kids. The more I did this, my thoughts seemed to stop running wild, like they knew I was watching them. The more my automatic narration quietened, the more my ego was able to be seen.

Given the right ingredients, the right situation, and my ego would show up in all its glory, lights and sirens flashing as the first responder. I began to keep a diary, writing down every time I was triggered, why, how I felt, what happened, and my thoughts. I noticed that my thoughts were like those of an overprotective parent or older sibling.

My ego made statements like:

'She should not speak to you like that.'
'He's taking advantage of you.'
'She does not like you.'
'You can't do that.'
'He doesn't care about you.'
'You can do better.'

I realised that when my ego came rushing into a situation, it was to protect me. It sounds strange that telling yourself that someone does not care is a protection method, but it is. If my ego tells me that someone does not care, then more than likely, I am not going to care back. If I did not have an unbalanced and overactive Ego, I would still treat that person with care because my actions reflect me. My ego would not want me to risk giving my care to someone that could potentially not return the same back. This experience may hurt my feelings. To remedy this, my ego gets in first and tries to influence the situation. The ego cycle is self-perpetuating, never really getting anywhere but travelling far.

The ego wants to balance and help protect; however, in its protection, we can be imprisoned. When our ego is in extreme parental mode (EPM), our interactions with other people become clouded in misunderstandings and ego-driven interpretations that only seek to keep us safe behind its wall. In staying safe, we become too afraid to go into anything unpleasant within ourselves; we never have the chance to do the healing work and continue to rely on the protection of our egos.

When we arrived in our new country, my ego convinced me that I could live without friends, and in fact, it convinced me that I did not like any people at all. The point was, I did want friends, but my ego was preparing me for the worst-case scenario, which was the fact that as an older and more reserved adult, I may never make friends.

One incident caused me alarm, concern and resulted in me concentrating on my relationship with my ego. I called this event 'the mop' incident.

My relationship with my mother-in-law was very strained when we moved to our new country; she would come over and stay for months on end. Without knowing she had become part of my trauma team. When my mother-in-law was in my home, I expected her to meet my expectations in line with everyone else. She was expected to be up and out of bed at the same time as us, spend the right amount of time with the kids while doing the right things with them. My mother-in-law was expected to help with cleaning and cooking. In any disagreements between her and me, my husband was expected to take my side over hers. I was still fully seated in my trauma and needed to maintain complete control of my home and family.

One day while my mother-in-law was over from our home country, I was mopping outside the furthest two bedrooms, which contained my eldest daughter in one and my mother-in-law in the other. It was twelve pm, and they were both still sleeping. As I vigorously scrubbed the floors, annoyance crept up behind me.

Looming over my shoulder, my ego whispered, 'they are taking advantage of you' I became angry that I was cleaning while others happily slept. As the pressure began to build up in my body, I looked down at the wet floor and back up to my mother-in-law's bedroom door. A thought entered my mind as I watched the door that was not my own. The thought said, 'if she slipped on the wet floor, it would serve her right.' I pumped the brake so hard that I nearly gave myself whiplash.

I knew that to find the underlying cause of this horrible thought I would need to drop the judgement. I braced myself and allowed the thoughts to travel through my mind freely. The thoughts said things such as:

'It would be karma if she slipped.'

'She would deserve it.'

'She disrespects you.'

I watched as these horrible thoughts passed me by and eventually asked my ego, *'are you done?'*

When my ego did not reply, I gathered the answer was yes. It was done with its rant. At first, there was disgust at what my ego had said, but then came compassion. I had a long talk with my ego and explained that the experiences that created its state of hypervigilance and overprotectiveness are over. I was safe now and loved.

This example shows just how easily your ego can spiral out of control. What is worse is that for years I believed these overprotective thoughts to be my own. People believe themselves to be the thoughts in their heads when they are not. The unfavourable ideas in their heads are the products of generation's worth of experience, conditioning, and manipulative protective behaviours, with the addition of protection software in our ego that keeps us from taking risks. That is why I see the ego as being the first responder because it is the first thing on the scene in anything that could potentially cause us emotional discomfort or pain.

CHAPTER TEN

✐

Turning Pain Into Peace

CREATING CONFIDENCE

We previously discussed ideas about what the ego is, and what it tries to achieve. It was always my ego, that was triggered in my painful moments, not the true me. If we want to reduce the frequency and intensity of triggering experiences (i.e., get rid of them), first, we need to build a relationship with the part of us that becomes triggered. A significant aspect of this process was building the ego's confidence in my ability to assess the danger in a situation.

The first step in this entire process, as detailed previously, was understanding the separation. The separation is understood when we start to observe our thoughts; we notice that they continue regardless. To create confidence in ourselves, we must enact that separation. We must keep that separation in mind as often as we can.

For example, someone tells you, that you are wrong.

.

Instead of letting your ego come charging in as the first responder, lights blaring, you take a step back in your mind; the ego still comes rushing in; however, this time, you are already there, waiting to see what it has to say. You and your ego are on the same team, so you take a few seconds to allow it to come through.

Usually, the ego would come rushing in, spilling straight out of your mouth, in a ball of emotion. But this time we are there. We listen to what it has to say, the concerns and worries. Those few seconds spent listening and observing our ego, gives us instant awareness and a reminder that we are separate.

On the outside, the few seconds spent watching the egos' reaction, creates enough space for us to be able to speak for ourselves. In this moment we do not let our egos talk for us, out of fear. We listen and honour the ego's voice, but we work towards not having it represent us in the outside world. When we enact the separation and make use of the space we have created, we can respond to a situation differently, whether right or wrong, the reaction chose would be ours to own.

In a reactionary situation, enacting the separation helps you to have objectivity. If your ego comes rushing in guns blazing, then you know it is in a heightened state. We also know that to soothe a heightened state, we need understanding. In the above scenario, had I not been present when my ego showed up, I may have reacted to that person in anger. Instead, I hear my ego in my mind say, 'they think you are stupid.' On hearing this, I thank my ego for the advice but tell it not to worry. My ego would be confused the first few times I did this, but eventually, it would sit back and relax. Speaking and thinking for myself means my ego can go into resting.

After creating space in my mind, I was able to use a tool that came naturally to me, talking. The talking was not with a person but my ego. I would get a piece of paper, and after a situation or an unnecessary reaction, I would do a counselling session with my ego. At the top, I would start with 'I feel.' Underneath, I would begin to pull out more information until we got to the base problem. The conversation would always boil down to fear. Even if my ego's thoughts and feelings seemed attacking, they would always eventually come back down to being scared.

If you feel like your ego is saying the same kind of things, continuously for different situations, I suggest taking time to go deeper into what the ego is trying to tell you. Coaching my ego took the form of a parent-child relationship. This structure was opposite, to how me and my ego had functioned previously. My ego had been the parent and myself the child. When I arrived at the point of being able to discuss alternative perspectives with my ego, I put forward my case, proving that I was safe, secure, loved, and listened to.

When coaching ourselves or our egos, it is critical that we remember to regularly assess our expectations. At the minimum, we should be doing this every time we embark on a new venture, relationship, or experience. This, along with resilience building, can minimise our triggers. If we do get triggered, we now know to spend time with our egos and ourselves.

The conversation below happened after I decided to take on home-schooling my children, for the first time, during an incredibly stressful period without checking in on my expectations first.

Me: How do you feel?
Ego: Disappointed in my kids.
Me: Why?
Ego: My kids reflect on me; they will make it look like I did a bad job teaching them.
Me: Really?
Me: No, I am not disappointed in them. I am disappointed in myself and my parenting.

Me: Why?
Ego: I am afraid that I am not going to be as good a teacher as I should be.
Me: Whose expectation is this?
Ego: My own.
Me: Really?
Me: No.
Me: Whose expectation is this?
Me: My dad's.

When I took on the challenge, I did not consider my need for perfection. I started to get frustrated with both myself and my kids. My ego thought that my kids did not care about the effort I had put into creating a unique curriculum, and the time I had sacrificed to deliver it. It was not that they did not care, they were just being kids, and I was just being triggered.

The base fear here was the fear of not meeting my dad's expectations. The old expectations of my dad had crept into the situation. It was what he would have expected from a home-schooling journey. If minor problems did arise with their home-schooling, with this awareness, if my ego came rushing in, I would know how to coach it.

The ability to enact the separation, by creating space gives us time to use different tools. It does not matter what books we read, if we cannot create space in our minds to use those tools. Enacting the separation (or becoming mindful) also prepared me to begin to learn meditation practices.

There are misconceptions regarding mindfulness and meditation. One being, which one comes first? It is said that mindfulness, comes with increased and committed meditation, my experience however, was contrary to this. My mindfulness practice not only came first but it also prepped my mind to transition into meditation. Meditation was a small part of my healing journey, usually only attempted when I had hit breaking point. My mindfulness practice, however, began as soon as I started to reflect, on where I was in my life and where I wanted to be. Mindfulness was present in the very beginning, in the practice of observing my thoughts. The more I could detach from my thoughts, in daily life, they could not interrupt me, and I could be present. The more present I was, the more beauty revealed itself in the mundane. If you are looking into meditation and mindfulness here are things to consider:

- You do not have to be able to stop thinking before trying to meditate.

- The aim of meditation is not to get rid of thoughts completely, nor straight away.

- Complicated meditation practices are not necessary, and are sometimes more of a distraction, than a tool.

- Merely sitting or lying quietly, while focusing on each breath as it travels through your body, in and out, is enough to create some peace.

- It may be more beneficial for you to learn mindfulness techniques, instead of, or alongside meditation. Especially, if you struggle with day-to-day thoughts and emotions. Mindfulness is underrated, in its application and usability. It can be done any time anywhere.

- If meditation is the tool that resonates with you, do not be discouraged to try, based on stereotypical ideals. The people we see engaging in these practices rarely look like us, they are either young and pristine in their techniques, or older wise gurus who have left normal life behind.

- Mindfulness and meditation create space for you, to be with you.

- As with any journey, mindfulness and meditation is one unique to you.

FORGIVENESS

In the past, when the word forgiveness was uttered, I would scoff. I always thought that to forgive someone, was to be letting that person off the hook; like me holding onto the negativity was their punishment. Forgiveness was the gift, given by those who were not consumed with trying to protect themselves. My personal thoughts on forgiveness echoed those of society; forgiveness was a sign of weakness.

If I did forgive, it was not done until it had been drawn out. In my eyes, quick forgiveness told the other person that you would happily put up with anything and everything. When someone has hurt you, betrayed you, lied to you, or just let you down, it is hard to move past the feelings that accompany those actions.

A big culprit in creating and maintaining those feelings is our egos and the protection that accompanies them. When someone lets us down or hurts us, the emotions are more intense because we are confused. We think we know what we should expect from someone, but we forget that the right way can be different for each human being. In Michael Newton's 'The Journey of Souls,' considerable research was done on people under hypnosis. He found that a significant percentage of those people examined described going to the same place in-between lives. Newton found that the research participants reviewed and selected their next lives based on what they were yet to learn. The number of research participants were in the thousands and were all unknown to each other.

When learning about concepts of the soul, afterlife, and reincarnation, I gained an understanding that, just like my thoughts, I was also not the things that happened to me. I know some people cannot and do want to understand their trauma, and rightfully so. Trauma can turn on switches that are hard to turn back off.

When I say I am not what happened to me, it means that dreadful things happened, things that should not happen to anyone, let alone a child, but that was not my story. It was my dad's. He was the one doing, inflicting, and my family and I were just the bodies. For me, this helped. It meant that I did not have to spend another few years asking, 'why me?' because there was no answer. I applied what I had learned about the soul's journey to my own childhood, removing the personalisation. My dad would receive consequences, and he knew it.

Being able to remove the personalisation of what was done to me released a heavy bag off my back. While we hold onto the pain and suffering that someone has caused us, it repeatedly plays. Meanwhile, the other person may not be suffering at all. Even if they can see the damage they have done, people may still not acknowledge it. Holding onto something is not beneficial at all. What is valuable is being able to let go. When I talk about forgiving, it does not have to be to the person's face; it does not have to be spoken. It must, however, be understood and excepted within yourself.

Terrible things happen to people every single day, every single minute. We must be able to forgive to move on. Forgiveness is for us, not for the other person that inflicts the pain. Feelings, emotions, and the body are all connected; everything that is negative that we hold on to manifests within our bodies as illness. We send out every word that we speak into the universe as energy, and we attract that same energy back. I decided to forgive my dad, early in my healing journey as I did not wish to hold onto it. I managed to try and understand the cycle of abuse he had been in and the mental health issues that he may have had as a result. It all helped me to let go. I did not tell anyone what I had done in forgiving him.

I am better than him. I committed to not letting the cycle of abuse continue for another generation, something he had not the strength to do. As hard as it had been facing my demons, I was doing it. The night that I decided to forgive him, I went to sleep, and for the first time in thirty-four years, I did not have a nightmare. It is not that my dad was not present in my dream. The dream now had a completely different feel. I was saving myself and my mum. I was no longer afraid. I played a different role now, I was more in control, and I was brave, and he, well, he was now an old man. In the process of forgiving him, I had taken his power away.

DIGGING UP DREAMS

After creating peace in my mind and environment, the next natural step was finding my purpose. I was nowhere near as peaceful then, as I am now, so do not assume that you must be 'fully healed', to start to think about these things. The fact is, there is no end; and no 'fully healed,' healing is a lifelong process, not a destination.

Surprisingly, I found that having something to focus on, outside of myself, contributed massively to my healing journey. When you embark on the project of finding 'you', instead of solely focusing on surviving 'you,' the pressure moves away from the inner struggle, and our attention shifts to the future and its possibilities. We start to focus on the outside world and where we can meaningfully fit within it.

It is hard to feel confident going into the public arena, especially after sometimes spending months, years, or decades navigating the fight of your life, with yourself. Unless it is an 'awareness' day, attitudes towards negative lived experiences are stuck in the dark ages. Only on awareness days can you be open about and celebrate things, such as surviving domestic violence or protecting children. Apart from those box-ticking special days, trauma is still taboo.

As I began to research and talk to people who have had negative lived experiences, I noticed increasingly that these people are primarily underappreciated, both in the public and professional arenas. What is worse is that these people know that, unless they aim for a specific not for profit that deals with the exact issues they have survived, their lived experience means nothing.

When I enter the professional and public world, I want to encourage people to change these attitudes. When you tell the average person a little about yourself, something that they would deem a negative life experience, their first reaction is to tilt their head to the side, pull their best sad face, and feel sorry for you. Empathy is great, but it should not come from a place of superiority, which is unfortunately sometimes where it comes from. Compassion should be empowering. It should say 'wow, you have been through a lot, and now you are thriving,' or 'wow, I wish I had your resilience.'

I have a friend to whom I really look up. She is an accomplished mental health nurse, an accountant, an amazing mother, daughter, and wife. This friend was humble and authentic. The first time I met her was random, in the middle of a noisy kids' play centre. I told her my whole, and I mean whole life story. She looked me deep in the eyes and said, "You have had a dramatic life," bear in mind that I had not even begun to realise that I needed to heal.

This statement by her was not condescending or pitiful. It was acknowledging and empowering. I left that conversation, thinking to myself that she was right. I had lived a dramatic life, but guess what? I was still here, and I smiled.

Before being forced to look at myself, I had consistently downplayed the things I had been through. My friend's comment was a positive seed. Over the years, we have very slowly built a friendship. It is not the kind where we see each other all the time; she is busy being a superwoman. I respect her for that. Luckily enough, my kids ended up at the same school as hers, so we have these intense passing hugs as we race through the school at drop-offs. We share quick words of love and continue with our lives. I know she is there for me, and I am there for her. The bond we have does not depend on anything.

This friend is relevant to this section because she said something that changed my confidence forever during our one and only coffee date. This woman was a mighty example of a female. I had so much respect and admiration for her. She had it all, she was doing it all, and she still exhumed love and compassion for everyone. During this catch up she blew me away; she told me that she looked up to me. I looked at her squinting my eyes in disbelief; how? Why would she look up to me? She explained that she admired how proactive I was, I saw a problem, and I acted upon it until it was better/solved.

It is not just our own insecurities, past conditioning, and the lack of value placed on negative life experiences, that we must overcome to find our purpose, but for those that are parents, it means letting go of our children a little. This is no easy feat. Even for a parent that has had a breeze of life, it is traumatic. The parent that has lived through abuse and trauma must battle extreme fear in letting go of their children even slightly. They know of the horrors this world can inflict, not just because of TV or the movies but also because of real life. Protecting my children has been a full-time job. At this point in life, I have trust in my own intuition. I am no longer making decisions in 'danger' mode. Because of this, I can begin the process of letting go, even if only very slightly.

Questions I asked myself to find my purpose

(Contrary to widely held belief, you do not have to find a purpose to fill your whole life, just the next phase of it. Your drive will evolve as you do)

Write the following questions on a piece of paper or in a journal and answer them. I have shared my answers with you.

1. If money were no object, what would you spend your time doing? (An old favourite, but an effective one in finding where your passion lies)

My Answers

I would have an enormous amount of land. It would be used as a safe place for childhood abuse and trauma survivors. Here they would be able to explore themselves, while making connections with others and creating a community of care.

2. What negative things have I experienced in this life? (This question gives us clues, about who our tribe is, those who can relate to us)

My Answers

Childhood trauma

Domestic Violence

Being let down by authorities; police/social services/school

Being let down by our community; neighbours/friends

Struggling to be a good mother

Low self-worth

Extreme menstruations

Poor physical health (overeating to self soothe)

3. What have you achieved to get through life? (This tells us, the teachability of our experience)

Teachability does not necessarily lead to teaching something. It can be creating a product or service that solves a part of an issue. For example, if I had been homeless and gained permanent residence, I could do workshops, to guide other homeless people in the process that worked for me.

There may be a specific part of being homeless that I have an idea for, like providing transport to get to interviews or an address to apply for jobs. Teachability to me is, understanding how I can use my experience to help others in a similar boat.

Try not limit this list to things such as career and qualifications, every time there is something we must get past to move forward, there is achievement. Try not to classify your achievements, because what is insignificant to you can be life changing for someone else.

My Answers

I have let go of societies time frames, of where I should be in life and what I should have.

I have become aware of how expectations that are not my own, influence my behaviour.

I am no longer an over-thinker.

I managed to become a more relaxed and peaceful mother.

I built my own self-worth up to the point of not allowing low self-confidence to stop me from moving forward in my goals.

I have learned to forgive, both people who have done me wrong and myself for the mistakes I had made.

I am learning to smile.

I am not so hard on myself anymore.

I can make healthier life choices.

4. In what situations do you feel you have a positive impact on people? Think about what people gain from you, intentionally or unintentionally. (This informs us of where our service to others lies)

My Answers

When I am listening to people, I am fully present in that moment. I am incredibly non-judgemental because I have a deep understanding of cycles and conditioning.

When I talk with people in general, I am told that I am helpful in my advice.

5. What is your purpose?

My Answers

Answer (2019): To help people that have been through painful situations, see that there is light at the end of the tunnel.

Answer Evolved (2020) To use writing, counselling, and workshops, to help people that have had trauma break negative cycles.

Answer Evolved (2021) To improve outcomes for both parents that have had trauma and their dependent children.

As you can see, the conclusion I came to has become more clearly expressed. The purpose is the underlying foundation of all your activities; the purpose is not a business idea or a job. It is, however, the driving force behind those things. Your ideas, career and projects lead to you fulfilling your purpose.

Parting Message

I hope to see a day very soon, when people that have been through traumas, big or small, are acknowledged for both their resilience and skills. Many of which can be applied to all areas of public and private life. I hope to see these people who are surviving and thriving after trauma, be raised up as the heroic examples they are.

We are not our circumstances, or the things that happen to us, but we are the healing.

Notes

- Arntz, W., Chasse, B. and Vicente, M., 2007. *What the bleep do we know?!*. Deerfield Beach, Fla.: Health Communications.

- Whatthebleep.com. 2022. *What the Bleep Do We Know!? | Stream the Bleep! Instantly!*. [online] Available at: <https://whatthebleep.com/shop/stream-the-bleep/> [Accessed 10 January 2022].

- Newton, M. (2019). *Journey of souls: case studies of life between lives*. Woodbury, Minnesota: Llewellyn Publications.
- Byrne, R. (2016). *The secret: the 10th anniversary edition*. New York, Ny: Atria Books; Hillsboro, Or.
- Mooji.org. (n.d.). *Mooji - Official Site*. [online] Available at: https://mooji.org/

Further Reading

- Tolle, E. (2004). *The power of NOW: a guide to spiritual enlightenment*. Vancouver, B.C.: Namaste Pub.; Novato, Calif.
- Tolle, E. (2016). *A new earth: awakening to your life's purpose*. New York: Plume.
- Neale Donald Walsch. (2014). *Conversations with God: an uncommon dialogue*. Charlottesville, Va: Hampton Roads Publishing.
- Foundation For Inner Peace (2008). *A Course in Miracles: Combined Volume*. Foundation For Inner Peace.

- Coelho, P. (1988). *The Alchemist.* New York Harper Collins Publishers.
- Redfield, J. (2018). *The celestine prophecy: an adventure.* New York: Grand Central Publishing.

www.ingramcontent.com/pod-product-compliance
Lightning Source LLC
Chambersburg PA
CBHW072047090426
42733CB00033B/2413